ECONOMIC INTEGRATION
IN LATIN AMERICA

ECONOMIC INTEGRATION
IN
LATIN AMERICA

The Progress and Problems of LAFTA

F. JOHN MATHIS

No. 8 in Studies in Latin American Business Series

BUREAU OF BUSINESS RESEARCH
THE UNIVERSITY OF TEXAS AT AUSTIN

1 9 6 9 $3.00

FOREWORD

The Bureau of Business Research is pleased to add *Economic Integration in Latin America: The Progress and Problems of Lafta* as Number 8 in its Studies in Latin American Business Series. This monograph highlights a subject of great interest to businessmen and economists in the United States. Dr. F. John Mathis of the State University of New York at Brockport, the author, is a specialist in the economy of Latin America. The manuscript was edited by Dr. Graham Blackstock. The cover was designed by Douglas Winters, and offset printing was done by Robert Dorsett and Daniel Rosas.

STANLEY A. ARBINGAST
Associate Director

June 1969

PREFACE

Asociación Latinoamericana de Libre Comercio is the most important undertaking in this decade, if not this century, for promotion of development within Latin America. It is the first step toward the establishment of a Latin American Common Market with unrestricted intrazonal trade, a common external tariff against third countries, and free mobility of the factors of production internally.[1] Although the time allotted to establish a common market has been set at fifteen years (1970–1985), according to the Declaration of Presidents' meeting in Punta del Este in 1967,[2] many major problems are yet to be solved. The purpose of this study is to point out the most pertinent problems, discuss proposed solutions, analyze their effectiveness, and in some cases suggest possible alternatives in situations where the solutions have not worked according to plan.

Earlier outstanding studies of economic integration in Latin America[3] have presented the background and examined integration developments up to about 1965. It is the design of this study to attempt to fill the gap from that year to the present. Unlike numerous other recent studies on Latin American economic integration which have concentrated on the Central American Common Market (CACM), this study is concerned with the Latin American Free Trade Association. LAFTA, primarily because of its physical, economic, and political importance, constitutes *the* organization that will determine the success or failure of the common market in Latin America.

Unlike recent writers who adopt a pessimistic attitude toward the success of LAFTA and the establishment of a common market,[4] the author of this study feels that significant progress has occurred, that many bottlenecks have been overcome, and that, although complete

[1] As defined by Bela Balassa, *The Theory of Economic Integration*, p. 2.

[2] For text see *U.S. Department of State Bulletin*, May 8, 1967, pp. 714–721.

[3] Sidney Dell, *A Latin American Common Market?* and Miguel S. Wionczek (ed.), *Latin American Economic Integration*.

[4] Roy Blough, Jack N. Behrman, and Romulo A. Ferrero, *Regional Integration and the Trade of Latin America*.

success is still in the distant future, LAFTA has come a long way since its inception.

In the process of writing this monograph the author received assistance from many people to whom he is indebted. I would like to thank Pan American Union for the grant which enabled me to spend several months doing research at LAFTA headquarters in Montevideo and at CACM headquarters in Guatemala. Special thanks for comments and suggestions are owing to Professor Walter Krause of the University of Iowa; Dr. Elba Kybal, chief, Technical Unit on Economic Integration, Pan American Union; Dr. Juan Bautista Schroeder, Pan American Union; Alberto Fabini, technical advisor on commercial policy, LAFTA; Dr. Juan José Real and Dr. Alfredo Blom Flor, of LAFTA; William A. Rosenthal and Juan Carlos Mira, of Business International; W. V. Turnage, special U.S. advisor on LAFTA affairs; Sr. Bernardo Soto Field, of the Secretaría Permanente del Tratado General de Integración Económica Centroamericana (SIECA), CACM; Dr. M. E. Bond, of Arizona State University; Richard Szal and James Doti; and my wife, Linda, for her editing suggestions and patience. I want to thank also Dr. Graham Blackstock, of the Bureau of Business Research, The University of Texas at Austin, whose editorial assistance was invaluable, and Dr. John R. Stockton, director of the Bureau, for giving me the opportunity to publish this study under Bureau auspices. The manuscript was written at the University of Illinois at Chicago before I accepted my present position.

F. JOHN MATHIS

State University of New York
College at Brockport
Brockport, New York

CONTENTS

LIST OF TABLES

xi

LIST OF FIGURES

LIST OF ABBREVIATIONS

ADC	Andean Development Corporation
AID	Agency for International Development
ALALC	Asociación Latinoamericana de Libre Comercio
CABEI	Central American Bank for Economic Integration
CACM	Central American Common Market
CIAP	Comití Interamericano de la Alianza para el Progreso (Inter-American Committee on the Alliance for Progress)
ECLA	Economic Commission for Latin America
EEC	European Economic Community
GATT	General Agreement on Tariffs and Trade
IA-ECOSOC	Inter-American Economic and Social Council
IBRD	International Bank for Reconstruction and Development
IDB	Inter-American Development Bank
IMF	International Monetary Fund
INTAL	Instituto para la Integración de América Latina (Institute for the Integration of Latin America)
LACM	Latin American Common Market
LAFTA	Latin American Free Trade Association
OAS	Organization of American States
ODECA	La Organización de los Estados Centroamericanos (The Organization of Central American States)
ROCAP	Regional Office for Central America and Panama
SIECA	Secretaría Permanente del Tratado General de Integración Económica Centroamericana
UN	United Nations
UNCTAD	United Nations Conference on Trade and Development

PART I

REGIONAL INTEGRATION IN LATIN AMERICA

RATIONALE

The majority of national markets in Latin America, very small in size and even smaller in terms of relatively low per capita income, cannot support the efficient operation of modern large-scale industry at or near full capacity. Even existing secondary industries are operating at a level significantly lower than full capacity. If Latin America did have large-scale industries, however, the goods they produced would have small export opportunity, since the markets of developed countries are closed to them because of high production costs, which are created by low labor productivity, absence of complementary facilities, and the technological lag.

Given limited access to both domestic and foreign markets, the case for the establishment of a common market is very convincing, since it provides access to a regional market that would create several possibilities: (1) existing productive capacity could be used more fully to supply the regional needs; (2) industries could reduce costs as a result of potential economies through expanded output and regional specialization; and (3) increased attractiveness for new investment arises as a result of the regional market area. The wider market permits the possibility of exploiting economies of scale with respect not only to the domestic market but also to the market in the developed country. On the domestic scene a protected regional market encourages additional investment in infant industries (whether import-substitution or export-creating) and although there is the danger of inefficiency, it is possible that with proper regulation these industries could become competitive in the world market. Nations becoming part of a more cohesive regional block, furthermore, would be in a more advantageous bargaining position.

Let us elaborate on some of the points mentioned in the preceding paragraph. A primary concern underlying regional economic integration is a more rational utilization of available resources and other factors of production to provide a better framework in which to meet the needs of the people within a region. Improved utilization would be fostered through both the promotion of a greater mobility of factors

3

and the creation of a wider market area. Greater intercountry movement of factors of production, as a prelude to output, helps to lower unit costs of production and to improve efficiency.

The motivation behind improving efficiency stems directly from the competition of freer trade within the region and competition of foreign firms investing in the region. Existing trade within the zone, which is directly at issue in the creation of a common-market area, is small relative to the total foreign trade of the individual participating countries. The trade liberalization associated with the creation of a common-market area should be evaluated not only as to its immediate impact upon the economies concerned, but also as to its potentialities as a lever which pries forth a sequence of events extending beyond any initial impact. The sequence involves additional output as wider markets arise within the region, improved efficiency resulting from additional output and realignment in activity, followed by added trade outside the region as the total competitive position of the region improves, accompanied by some realignment in export-import relationships between the region and the countries outside it.

This leverage effect is especially evident in the manner in which the stage is set for a somewhat altered pattern of production. That is, greater efficiency encourages greater sales, output, and income in two ways. First, greater sales within the region in terms of import substitution and volume in excess of that in existing import patterns become a possibility as more advantageous combinations of factors of production and lower unit costs come to prevail with reduced product prices. Furthermore, the establishment of a common market increases intrazonal trade, reducing the high dependence on imports, as trade barriers between the member countries fall and a common external tariff is established. Second, greater sales outside the region become a possibility as economic strength within the region is augmented relative to its trading relationships with countries outside the common-market area. With respect to foreign trade, the establishment of a common market could help to diversify export concentration because of the inducement to invest as a result of economies of scale. The diversification of export concentration has the added benefit of substantially removing the threat of fluctuations in the world market for primary commodities—a perennial worry of most developing countries. For these reasons, emphasis in an appraisal of a common market should

4

be placed primarily on growth, not merely on a reshuffling of what already exists.

Another opportunity presented by a common market is the development of industrial exports which could be sent to the other countries of the region in exchange for products which otherwise would have necessitated domestic production. Thus, instead of establishing numerous import-substitution industries, each country could specialize in production best suited to its national resources and resort to imports from other areas of Latin America to satisfy requirements which cannot be met by purchases from outside the region because of the shortage of foreign exchange. In general then, the gradual establishment of a common market implies that the decrease in the coefficient of imports from the rest of the world, which results from the relatively slow growth of primary exports, can be partially offset by an increase in the coefficient of intraregional imports from other Latin American countries.

One of the most important justifications for establishment of a common market is the inducement it provides foreign investment to flow into the region. This emphasis arises as a consequence of the threat of currently stagnating and possibly decreasing foreign-aid allotments from developed countries, rising debt-service costs on previously borrowed funds, and prolonged problems associated with the developing countries' foreign-trade dependence. The incentive for foreign investment to flow into the region, in place of continued trade from outside, comes from the establishment of a common external tariff barrier protecting the regional market. The resulting competition of regional products will induce foreign firms to reevaluate their position regarding the best location of the industry to supply the common-market area. This inflow of foreign private capital and business knowledge is believed necessary to stimulate economic development in Latin America.

The foregoing results are somewhat contrary to those presented by Jacob Viner in *The Customs Union Issue.* Viner argues that the primary purpose of a customs union is to shift production either to lower-cost or to higher-cost sources of supply. He argues that the advantages and disadvantages of a customs union are determined by the amount of trade created or diverted. In the case of underdeveloped countries a customs union would result in shifts from low-cost sources of supply for manufactures in industrial countries to high-cost sources within the underdeveloped countries. According to Viner, underdeveloped countries do not carry on a large amount of intrazonal trade and, therefore, do not benefit from participating in a customs union unless there is a large amount of trade between countries.

A major problem with Viner's analysis is its concern with the problem of optimal allocation of given resources under fixed conditions of production and competition. It is unrealistic to assume that in an underdeveloped country resources or conditions of production are fixed, since immobility of factors prevents competitive forces from operating effectively. Therefore Viner's analysis does not apply to the formation of a common market among underdeveloped countries.

A leading proponent of regional integration is Raul Prebisch. His rationale is based on the criticism of the law of comparative advantage, which he believes is "out-dated by reality" and continues to work only to the technological detriment of the underdeveloped countries in the sense of perpetuating the status quo.[1] The pattern of trade that has developed is such that one or two major export products represent 80–90 percent of export receipts and account for a very large proportion of GNP. Prebisch therefore argues that any small fluctuation in demand for these products has drastic effects on income and employment in the underdeveloped countries. He also points out peculiar problems in the demand and supply of exports of the underdeveloped countries. The excess supply of these primary exports keeps their price low, thus limiting revenues and, if the supply is increased, the price falls, further depressing revenues. On the other hand, if output is restricted the price does not rise, because of inelastic demand for these exports and the competition from synthetics as substitutes. These damaging conditions persist while the import demand in underdeveloped countries continues to increase rapidly. The gap of imports over exports is worsened by a deteriorating trend in the terms of trade unfavorable to the exports of the underdeveloped countries.

Prebisch' solution lies with industrialization, which he feels can best be facilitated through regional integration and the eventual establishment of a common market. Industrialization is a complex problem, especially when faced with competition from the industries of the more

[1] See UN, *The Economic Development of Latin America and Its Principal Problems.*

developed countries. The answer according to Prebisch is industries of the import-substitution type which are oriented to producing goods that can substitute for the increasing imports demanded and, since the goods were previously imported, a market is guaranteed. Integration—through the development of intrazonal trade—would expand this domestic market, and a common external tariff would protect the infant industries. Regional integration has other benefits in terms of reduced production costs resulting from economies of scale and more efficient-sized plants than narrow domestic markets permit. Recently Prebisch shifted emphasis from import substitution to the establishment of export-creating industries, which also are helped by the existence of a common market. These industries represent the ultimate steps in the diversification of export concentration for the underdeveloped countries.

A promoting factor for regional integration was the decline in intrazonal trade among LAFTA countries, from about 12 percent of total imports in 1953 to about 7 percent in 1961. While this represented a 25-percent decline in intrazonal trade, imports from the rest of the world increased by more than 20 percent. The cumulative average annual rate of growth fell in areas other than trade. Although relatively high rates of increase for Latin America occurred during 1945–1955 in per capita product (2.7 percent) and in per capita income (3.3 percent), in 1955–1958 the figures fell to 1.1 and 0.5 percent, respectively. This reinforced further the arguments in favor of regional integration.[2]

This perspective on the rationale for economic integration should make more meaningful the circumstances under which LAFTA was actually formed.

[2] See Sidney Dell, *A Latin American Common Market?* Chapter II, pp. 15–34.

HISTORICAL BACKGROUND

The years since World War II witnessed a pronounced movement throughout much of the world toward regional approaches as avenues of solution to particular pressing problems. A regional approach was employed, to an important extent, by Western Europe in the promotion of its economic recovery following World War II. The Marshall Plan, for example, stressed an overall multicountry attack upon the general economic inadequacies characteristic of a group of countries. This regional emphasis was thereafter continued in particularized connections—as various additional or supplementary matters came to be dealt with. The final result was the establishment of the European Economic Community (EEC).

Less developed countries also came to look to regional approaches, particularly as a means for promoting economic development and growth at a more rapid rate and along more rational lines than otherwise seemed likely or possible. Indeed, the United States government, through foreign economic assistance, came to favor regional approaches for solving problems of development—as evidenced, in part, by the establishment of its special Asian Development Fund (1956) and in subsequent endorsement of the Inter-American Development Bank (1958).[1]

Early Organizations

The growing emphasis upon regional approaches extended also to Latin America. In the realm of commercial trade two major developments bear mentioning. The Central American Common Market (CACM), comprising five Central American countries—Costa Rica, El Salvador, Guatemala, Honduras, and Nicaragua—has a long history of attempts at political integration. In 1951 the foreign ministers of the five countries signed the Charter of San Salvador, establishing the Organization of Central American States (La Organización de los

[1] For an earlier appraisal along these lines see Walter Krause, *The Impact of Latin American Common Markets on the Economies of Member States of the Organization of American States.*

8

Estados Centroamericanos) aimed at the consolidation of Central American activities. The same year the first steps toward economic integration were taken when the Economic Commission for Latin America (ECLA) approved the establishment of the Central American Economic Cooperation Committee. Their purpose was to direct the economic development of the area by promoting a gradual integration of the member countries, thus leading to higher levels of productivity and real income.

In 1958, after several years of study and negotiation by ECLA, the five countries signed the Multilateral Treaty of Central American Free Trade and Economic Integration, effective 1959, and the Agreement on the Regime for Central American Integration Industries, effective 1963. The Multilateral Treaty called for the establishment of a free-trade area and a customs union within a ten-year period encompassing equalization in the treatment of regionally traded goods and the elimination of export subsidies. The Central American Agreement on Equalization of Import Duties and Charges, signed in 1959, elaborates upon this treaty and provides for the establishment of a common external tariff within five years.

The General Treaty on Central American Economic Integration, or the "Managua Treaty," which supersedes all previous integration agreements, contained the following major provisions: (1) a Central American Common Market to be established within five years with all products freed from duties or other restrictions, except for a special list of exempted items, (2) a common treatment of goods by all countries in intraregional trade, (3) a standardization of laws relating to investment and industrial development, (4) a special agreement providing for a Central American Bank for Economic Integration (CABEI) to serve as the regional financing agency in promoting regional economic development, and (5) administrative machinery and other means for settling possible disputes. Later agreements provided for a clearing house to reduce the need for effecting settlement in hard currencies and for the establishment of a common currency.

The Latin American Free Trade Association (LAFTA)

The formation of the Latin American Free Trade Association began in 1956 with the establishment of a Trade Committee under the direc-

9

tion of the Economic Commission for Latin America (ECLA) to study the mechanics of establishing a Latin American Common Market (LACM). In 1957 the Organization of American States held a meeting of Latin American finance ministers, who worked out the basic principles and resolutions of LAFTA. In 1959 Argentina, Brazil, Chile, and Uruguay began the process of establishing a free-trade zone among themselves, and with ECLA's persuasion Bolivia, Paraguay, Peru, Mexico, and Venezuela joined the negotiations of the Southern Zone.

In 1960 the Treaty of Montevideo, setting up a free-trade area, was signed by Argentina, Brazil, Chile, Mexico, Paraguay, Peru, and Uruguay. Shortly thereafter Ecuador and Colombia joined the Association. This brief and flexible treaty emphasized two major ways of accelerating economic development: (1) a gradual elimination of barriers to intraregional trade, and (2) the establishment, gradually and progressively, of a LACM. To reach these goals the Treaty contained the following major provisions:

1. A twelve-year program for trade liberalization which would eliminate all tariffs and other restrictions on imports of goods originating in the member countries. This is to be accomplished through: (a) a National List of imports for each member country, for which the country would make annual reductions of duties and restrictions equivalent to not less than 8 percent of the weighted average applicable to third countries, until these barriers are eliminated in respect of substantially all of the nation's imports from the area, and (b) a Common List consisting of products currently traded on which the member countries collectively agree to completely eliminate duties and other restrictions by 1973 and which shall constitute in terms of the aggregate value of the trade among the member countries not less than 25 percent of traded items negotiated every three years beginning in 1961. While a country's concession on items in the National List can be removed, this is not true for items on the Common List.

2. Expansion of trade and economic complementarity to promote closer coordination of the corresponding industrialization policies and mutual agreements on complementarity by industrial sectors.

3. Most-favored-nation treatment extending any benefits between two countries to all member countries.

4. Treatment in respect to internal taxation on products originating in the area to be no less favorable than that accorded to similar national products.

5. Permission of saving clauses that allow a member to impose non-discriminatory restrictions on imports of products included in the liberalization program if these are imported in such quantities that they are likely to have serious repercussions on specific industries vital to the national economy.

6. Special provisions relative to agriculture permitting a member country to institute appropriate nondiscriminatory measures designed to: (a) limit imports to the amount required to meet the deficit in internal production, and (b) equalize the prices of the imported and the domestic product, provided that no lowering of its customary consumption or increase in uneconomic production is involved.

7. Special measures in favor of the countries at a relatively less advanced stage of economic development.

8. Institutions and administrative organs—Conference of Contracting Parties and Executive Committee—to execute and supervise the implementation of the provisions of the Treaty and study the results.

Later agreements or resolutions established provisions for an intrazonal payment system in 1964, and a Council of Ministers to serve as the new head of LAFTA in 1965. In 1967 Venezuela officially joined LAFTA and by 1968 negotiations with Bolivia were well advanced.

PROBLEMS

The purpose of this study is to analyze the recent problems encountered and the progress achieved along the path toward the eventual establishment of a Latin American Common Market (LACM). These problems can be categorized into the following two classes: (1) internal problems related to the individual country's development effort and (2) problems of a general nature affecting all Latin America. Let us briefly examine each of these categories.

Problems of Individual Countries

It is often easy for those who have not visited the countries of Latin America to think of them mistakenly as essentially similar, differing only in political or natural boundaries. While it is true that all the Latin American countries are underdeveloped, they are definitely not equal in this respect, as illustrated by LAFTA's classification of countries into three groups: (1) Argentina, Brazil, and Mexico—the most developed countries; (2) Colombia, Chile, Peru, Uruguay,[1] and Venezuela—countries in the insufficient-market category; and (3) Bolivia, Ecuador, and Paraguay—the relatively less developed countries.[2]

In Tables 1 and 2 the countries have been separated according to their status as more developed and less developed. Table 1 shows the great diversity in market size between the two groups. Argentina, Brazil, and Mexico together account for about 55 percent of the total land of Latin America, 64 percent of the population, and nearly 65 percent of the gross national product in 1967. The corresponding percentages with respect to LAFTA are 69, 71, and 69 percent. The average per capita income in 1967 for the more developed countries

[1] At a recent Council of Ministers meeting (1967) Uruguay was reclassified as a relatively less developed country until 1972.

[2] Throughout this study the less developed countries refer to the following LAFTA countries: Chile, Colombia, Peru, Uruguay, Venezuela, Bolivia, Ecuador, and Paraguay.

Table 1

GENERAL DATA SHOWING DIVERSITY AMONG
LATIN AMERICAN COUNTRIES

	1 Area (sq. miles)	2 Population est. 1967 (thousands)	3 GNP 1967 (mill. $U.S.)	4 Per capita GNP 1967 ($U.S.)
LAFTA				
Argentina	1,072,069	23,255	15,890	685
Brazil	3,286,478	85,655	22,750	267
Mexico	761,601	45,671	20,750	460
Chile	286,396	8,970	4,510	501
Colombia	439,513	19,191	5,410	284
Peru	496,222	12,385	4,540	370
Uruguay	72,172	2,783	1,567	565
Venezuela	352,143	9,352	8,075	875
Bolivia[1]	423,163	3,801	632	160
Ecuador	104,505	5,508	1,175	217
Paraguay	137,047	2,161	461	216
CACM				
Costa Rica	19,575	1,594	632	396
El Salvador	8,259	3,151	840	270
Guatemala	42,042	4,717	1,500	315
Honduras	43,246	2,445	535	223
Nicaragua	53,938	1,783	622	351
Panama[1]	29,208	1,329	660	503
OTHER				
Dominican Republic	18,816	3,889	990	259
Haiti	10,714	4,581	361	76

[1] Unofficial member of the organization.

Source: Column 1 from UCLA (Latin American Center), *Statistical Abstract of Latin America, 1965* (California: 1966); Column 2 from UN, *Monthly Bulletin of Statistics* (New York: September 1968); Columns 3 and 4 from Agency for International Development, Statistics and Reports Division.

was $470, as compared to an average of $398 for the less developed countries of LAFTA and $348 for all Latin America. For select industrial sectors, Argentina, Brazil, and Mexico in 1965 account for 62 percent of the cement production, 83 percent of the crude steel manufactured, and 67 percent of electrical-energy production. Analogous percentages with respect to LAFTA are 65, 83, and 70 percent. Transportation in Latin America also illustrates the predominant role

TABLE 2

SELECT INDUSTRIAL AND TRANSPORTATION DATA FOR LATIN AMERICA, 1965

	1 Cement production (thousands metric tons)	2 Crude steel production (thousands metric tons)	3 Elect. energy production (mill. kwh)	4 Motor vehicles (thousands)	5 Paved roads (miles)	6 Railroads (thousands of miles)	7 Air transport (mill. of tons/mile)	8 Merchant fleet (thous. of gross tons)
LAFTA								
Argentina	3,305	1,360	14,700	1,378	36,656	70.6	141.7	1,464
Brazil	5,545	2,896	30,128	1,784	30,136	60.3	418.5	1,684
Mexico	4,322	2,403	17,769	1,082	54,279	39.2	185.6	444
Chile	1,188	441	6,131	188	5,370	13.3	66.4	353
Colombia	2,053	204	6,000	224	9,684	5.6	184.7	201
Peru	1,023	81	3,808	209	7,935	5.3	39.2	222
Uruguay	431	12	1,649	200	4,402	4.8	10.2	15
Venezuela	2,112	625	8,171	498	21,271	0.4	79.0	448
Bolivia[1]	60	…	568	44	989	5.6	7.2	…
Ecuador	325	…	590	40	2,379	1.9	7.5	43
Paraguay	29	…	188	18	539	1.9	3.5	20
CACM								
Costa Rica	…	…	670	39	1,768	1.4	23.8	92
El Salvador	81	…	410	31	1,699	0.9	18.3	…
Guatemala	231	…	480	52	2,408	1.2	9.0	…
Honduras	94	…	180	16	613	2.0	12.8	90
Nicaragua	66	…	320	17	1,304	0.6	7.2	…
Panama[1]	165	…	450	37	1,708	0.4	12.8	…
OTHER								
Dominican Republic	212	…	640	30	6,849	2.0	1.6	27
Haiti	42	…	110	10	678	0.8	…	…

[1] Unofficial member of the organization.

Source: Columns 1 to 3 from UCLA (Latin American Center), *Statistical Abstract of Latin America, 1965* (California: 1966); Columns 4 to 8 from Agency for International Development, Statistics and Reports Division, and Pan American Union, Statistical Office.

of the three, which have 72 percent of all motor vehicles, 64 percent of the paved roads, 78 percent of the railroad mileage, 61 percent of the air transportation, and 70 percent of the merchant-fleet tonnage. Again, parallel percentages with respect to LAFTA are 75, 70, 81, 65, and 73 percent.

The wide diversity among countries is also reflected by the peculiar problems facing individual countries. Many of the problems can be classified under these general headings: political instability, bureaucracy and public employment, inequality of land tenure, inflation and exchange instability, inadequate foreign exchange and balance-of-payments problems, insufficient and inequitable tax systems, under-employment and unemployment, and insufficient markets. In reality, however, the general problem becomes a special problem in each country, peculiar to it because of its cultural and social characteristics, traditions, history, and political attitudes. For example, Brazil, Mexico, El Salvador, Honduras, Nicaragua, Dominican Republic, and Haiti are countries with greater than 56 percent of the labor force in agriculture as compared to 12 percent for the United States. The percentages of total exports earnings derived from one commodity in 1964 were as follows: Brazil 53 percent (coffee), Chile 59 percent (copper), Colombia 73 percent (coffee), Venezuela 93 percent (petroleum), and Bolivia 72 percent (tin). Between 1956 and 1965 Argentina, Brazil, Chile, and Bolivia had rampant inflationary problems.

In Argentina the inflation problem has been encouraged by an average annual rise of 22 percent in the official rate of exchange and significant increases in money wages. Development is continually hampered by the burden of servicing the debt. Extremely high inflation in Brazil is the primary problem, but it is related to the problem of a net deficit in public income and expenditure because of the pressure to develop and the dependence on one export product. The main problems in Mexico are said to result from demand-pull pressures on prices and balance-of-payments deficits. Chile, characterized by chronic economic disequilibrium, inflation, and rising government deficits, is also threatened by growing social pressures and their political expression. Colombia has been plagued with a highly volatile growth rate caused by structural obstacles, changes in the export sector, decline in gross investment, rising government deficit, and monetary instability. Cur-

15

rently Uruguay is suffering from strong inflationary pressures related to the long process of economic stagnation and instability, a rigidity of agricultural supplies, currency devaluation, balance-of-payments problems, social pressures and labor disputes, and a narrow market. Venezuela has had an appreciable deterioration in the terms of trade, overly high export concentration, and slow growth in the volume of exports. Bolivia's problem stems from the close ties of the economy to tin exports. Moreover, the continued rise in public expenditure to overcome the increasing unemployment problem has caused inflation. Finally, Paraguay's progress is hindered by the fact that a larger part of the population are in the subsistence sector and by the lack of an export market.[3] Hence, the movement toward a Latin American Common Market (LACM) is faced with a broad spectrum of economies with extreme physical diversity and problem disparity. These disparities are further widened by national jealousies and military accusations and fears, as seen in recent months.

Although the main concern of this study is not the particular problems of individual countries and their solution, the fact cannot be overlooked that these problems and all integration efforts directly affect each other. For example, the integration agreements and policies have been accepted by the foreign ministers or high government officials, but these policies are executed or implemented at a much lower level—the level of the customs officer, dock official, or other low-level national (not international) government employee.

Problems of Latin America

The problems faced by Latin America are related to the general level of development of the area in terms of the development level of other countries of the world. Their solution, on the basis of recent thinking and history, is contingent on solutions to the problems facing the establishment of a LACM. Until very recently most of the talk of a LACM was generated by the Economic Commission for Latin America (ECLA), which carried out much of the ground work for the Central American Common Market (CACM) and the Latin American Free Trade Association (LAFTA). In the past a LACM was a reality only in

[3] The main source of information for this paragraph is UN, *Economic Survey of Latin America*, 1965.

16

the minds of the theoreticians, and little more than a dream to most leading officials. The basic reason for this attitude was the distinct individual differences among the Latin American countries.

The precise form of the dream for Latin America did not begin to emerge until the signing of the Treaty of Montevideo in 1960. But it was not until 1965 and the creation of the Council of Ministers of LAFTA that the dream began to assume reality. Previously all agreements negotiated by the various national representatives to LAFTA were subject to approval by the individual national governments, which met separately and not under LAFTA auspices. Thus months of cooperation by the representatives could be nullified by the national governments. The real test of the degree to which national differences can be overcome will depend on the power and effectiveness of the Council of Ministers.

Whereas the European Economic Community (EEC) was formed by countries that had an established industrial infrastructure and were economically developed, the countries of Latin America were just beginning to develop. Further unlike the situation of the European countries, the Latin American countries were at different stages in this development process. While the EEC member countries had developed extensive relations among themselves prior to integration, the Latin American countries, producing and trading similar goods, had constructed substantial trade barriers against one another to protect their domestic markets. As a result, industrial development proceeded within the limitations of existing national markets. Industries not oriented toward selling specifically in their own national market sold to the foreign market outside Latin America. Thus, there was a dual problem of reorienting the existing national industries toward selling in a regional market, and improving the efficiency of these national industries so that they could compete regionally.

Somewhat related to the above problem, and again unlike the situation of the European Economic Community, was Latin America's necessity for creating entirely new channels of trade and financing, commercial contacts, clearing and payment mechanisms, sources of supply, and market outlets. This task appears rather acute when one considers the poor transportation and communication systems *within* a particular country; it seems almost ridiculously impossible when viewed in the context of the situation *between* different countries.

These physical problems are compounded by policy barriers, such as the many and varied ramifications of tariffs and other restrictions controlling trade between countries. One must also take into consideration the various exchange rates, which are continually subject to inflationary pressures and revaluation.

Development planning, until very recently, has been integrated in no way on a regional basis. Now there is some attempt to coordinate the plans of individual countries through a board of nine members, under the auspices of the Organization of American States (OAS). The few participating countries submit their national plans to the board, which coordinates them on a regional basis and formulates a regional plan. Foreign aid to Latin America also has been distributed on a country-by-country basis, rather than in a regional context.[4] Of course, any attempt to establish a common market requires some degree of coordination of the national economies and policies toward third countries.

The solution of these problems depends on the success of LAFTA and its establishment of a free-trade area, subsequently a customs union, and finally, a common market. With this we turn to the problems facing LAFTA and the progress being made toward their solution, which are directly related to the problems facing all Latin America, and indirectly connected with solving the development bottlenecks in each country. A descriptive analysis of these problems and current progress toward their solution is discussed in the following section.

[4] The U.S. Aid program for CACM, besides having national offices, also has a regional office of the Agency for International Development—Regional Office for Central America and Panama (ROCAP)—located in Guatemala. Technical and financial assistance is given on a regional basis to members of CACM.

PART II
THE CURRENT JUNCTURE

LAFTA: THE DRIVING FORCE

It is obvious that the Latin American Free Trade Association, rather than the Central American Common Market, is the forerunner of the Latin American Common Market. Even though CACM is well ahead of LAFTA in the establishment of a common market, one cannot overlook the fact that the LAFTA countries account for over 90 percent of Latin America's area, population, GNP, industrial investment, and exports and imports. This is not to say, however, that LAFTA cannot learn organizational procedures from CACM in the process of developing LACM.

At the recent meeting of American Presidents and in the resulting Declaration of April 1967,[1] it was emphasized that the two organizations should cooperate to further the establishment of a LACM. As a result, LAFTA established an ad-hoc commission composed of the Executive Secretary of LAFTA and three other permanent representatives of the Contracting Parties.[2] The purposes of this ad-hoc commission were several: (a) to exchange information with the pertinent CACM representative on matters indicated by the Permanent Executive Committee of LAFTA, (b) to inform the Committee on all those aspects that were suggested by the representative authority, (c) to submit the framework for the constitution of the mixed LAFTA-CACM Commission for the Committee's coordination, and (d) to present a report to the Committee covering the results of its work which will be brought to the attention of the next Council of Ministers' meeting.

During late July the ad-hoc commission and LAFTA's Executive Secretary, Gustavo Magarinos, met with CACM authorities to discuss these points. As a result of this meeting a Coordinating Commission of LAFTA

[1] For text see *U.S. Department of State Bulletin*, May 8, 1967, pp. 714–721.

[2] See Resolution 123 of the LAFTA Permanent Executive Committee. Previously, in December 1966, the Council of Ministers of LAFTA had recommended to the Permanent Executive Committee the establishment of channels of continuous communication with the corresponding organs of CACM. They also encouraged the study of the possibility of granting nonreciprocal tariff preferences to the countries of Central America and Panama to encourage the integration of both systems.

21

and CACM was established to encourage Latin American integration.[3] It was also agreed that nonmember countries of LAFTA or CACM would be invited to participate in Commission meetings. The Commission's projected purpose was to carry out studies and formulate recommendations to facilitate the process of converging the two existing systems of integration as laid out earlier in Chapter I, Number 4, of the Declaration of Presidents. The composition of the Commission was set at eighteen persons—the five permanent representatives of the Executive Council for CACM, the eleven permanent representatives of the Permanent Executive Committee of LAFTA, and the Executive Secretaries of both organizations.

[3] LAFTA, Cómite Ejecutivo Permanente, *Acta de la Reunión de la Comisión Ad-Hoc de la Asociación Latinoamericana de Libre Comercio y los Organos Ejecutivos del Mercado Común Centroamericano*, CEP/Repartido 871, 1967.

EXECUTIVE AND INSTITUTIONAL PROBLEMS

As mentioned earlier, the Council of Ministers was created in 1965 to end the lack of a real executive power at the ministerial level of the member countries to implement the agreements proposed by LAFTA. The Council of Ministers, the supreme organ of LAFTA, has the following functions: (1) to establish general norms to complement the objectives of the Treaty and insure a harmonious process of economic and social development and integration, (2) to evaluate the efforts of the Association and establish the fundamental objectives to serve as the base for a program of work, (3) to identify and resolve major policy issues and to serve as a referee between the Conference and the Committee, (4) to establish basic norms to regulate the relation of the Association with countries outside the region and with international organizations, (5) to delegate to the Conference or Committee the power to make decisions on specific matters destined to permit more complementarity among the objectives of the Treaty, (6) to make decisions on amendments to the Treaty, (7) to modify the system of voting of the Conference, and (8) to establish procedural regulations.[1]

The Council of Ministers met for the first time at the end of 1966. It was criticized by Chile for its action at that meeting because it did not take more vigorous steps, while Argentina expressed satisfaction with the more cautious approach adopted. The most important decision of the meeting was the approval of a resolution for the Permanent Executive Committee to prepare a study concerning the use of automatic tariff reductions to replace the item-by-item negotiations currently used to reduce tariffs on intrazonal trade. One possibility considered was for different countries to have different automatic rates of reductions. If tariff reductions were made automatic—for example, if tariffs must be reduced by a certain percentage each year—this provision, LAFTA observers felt, would overcome the problem of annual negotiations for the elimination of obstacles. The automatic reductions would increase the number of trade concessions which decrease each year.

---

[1] LAFTA, *Sintesis Mensual*, January 1967, pp. 21–25.

Those in opposition to automatic reductions feel they would eliminate or greatly reduce the influence of the sectoral meetings.[2]

The Council of Ministers meeting between August 28 and September 2, 1967, was again somewhat disappointing to many. It was generally felt by interested parties that the true face of the Council would show itself at this meeting and thus establish the rate at which LAFTA would move to solve its current problems as a free-trade area and to develop a common market within the framework provided in the Declaration of Presidents. Although the meeting got off to a favorable start, it quickly ran into bottlenecks caused by disagreements between the relatively more developed and relatively less developed countries. The fundamental problem, which will not easily be overcome for some time, is the wide diversities among the member countries of LAFTA and, therefore, the wide diversity of their economic demands. A significant difference is apparent also in a comparison of the Council of Ministers of LAFTA to the similar council in CACM. The majority of the ministers of LAFTA are Ministers of Foreign Relations, with only one, the minister from Ecuador, being a Minister of Industry and Commerce, whereas in CACM, the members of the Council are the economic ministers of the various economies and, therefore, better qualified to decide what is needed for their country. At the same time they can better determine their countries' needs and benefits in a regional context. In CACM the majority of the issues considered at their Council of Ministers meeting are circulated, discussed, and generally agreed upon before the meeting ever begins.

In general, the problems at the administrative level seem to be related to the fact that adequate provision was made within the LAFTA organization for the examination of problems at the working level, but little of this seems to be translated into action plans for the member countries. This relates to the need for a more powerful central institution for executing development and integration activities among the member countries. Also lacking is an effective central planning organization to examine regional growth. Basically the problem is two-sided: on the one hand, LAFTA provides no machinery which carries

[2] While there has been a marked trend to rely more and more on the recommendations of the sectoral meeting for tariff concessions, as witnessed in 1966, this source of concessions alone is inadequate to maintain the early momentum of LAFTA in this area.

sufficient weight in national governments, and, on the other hand, national governments continue to think along near-autarkic lines, thus withholding their support of integration until concessions are first made by other countries.

A solution to this problem of an absence of a strong political head to guide LAFTA is not readily seen. To the extent that a solution is possible it will likely come only after each individual member of LAFTA decides to support regional integration completely. This requires a relaxing of the bonds of nationalism in favor of regionalism. Since this nationalistic feeling is "a part of the people" it presumably can be modified only by changing the attitude of the population toward regionalism. Under existing circumstances, therefore, it appears that it will be a number of years before the member countries decide, or become able, to give the Council of Ministers the power and support needed to comprise an effective policy-making body directing Latin American regional integration.

Other organs to be created in the future are: (1) a Court of Justice, (2) a Parliamentary liaison, and (3) a Technical Commission. The specific functions of the first two organs have not yet been presented. Regarding the Technical Commission, Resolution 118 (V) of the Conference[3] sets forth some general preliminary functions which were reviewed at the 1967 Council of Ministers meeting. Briefly, it is designated to be a regional-development planning organ composed of four leading economists; it will undertake studies, formulate proposals, and present projects to accelerate economic and social integration.

The following schematic diagram (Figure 1) shows the interrelationship of the various organizations of LAFTA. It should be pointed out that the private sector as well as the public sector of the member countries is represented in the organization.[4]

So far we have mentioned two major problems of LAFTA today—the lack of a real executive power at the ministerial level and the need for

[3] LAFTA (Conferencia), *Resoluciones*, 1966, pp. 119–120.

[4] The private-sector influence is felt in the sectoral meetings which decide upon items on which the tariff will or will not be reduced and which will be submitted for inclusion in the National Lists. Most of the 1966 trade concessions were a direct result of recommendations of the industry sectoral meetings. For example, of the 370 new products added to the National Lists, 293 (about 80 percent) were recommended by the industrial sectorals. However, the 293 concessions adopted represent only about one third of the total number of concessions (944) suggested by the sectorals.

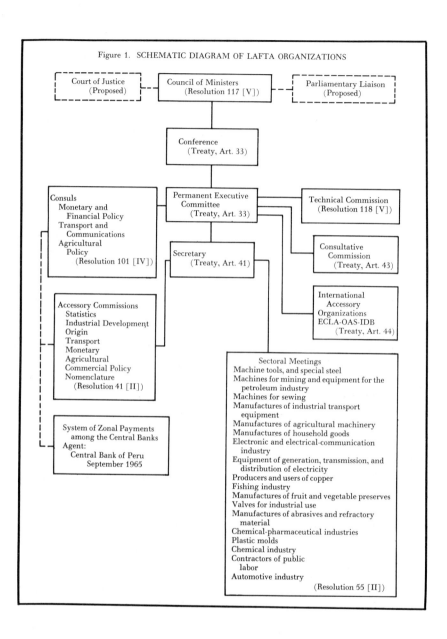

Figure 1. SCHEMATIC DIAGRAM OF LAFTA ORGANIZATIONS

Court of Justice
(Proposed)

Council of Ministers
(Resolution 117 [V])

Parliamentary Liaison
(Proposed)

Conference
(Treaty, Art. 33)

Consuls
    Monetary and
        Financial Policy
    Transport and
        Communications
    Agricultural
        Policy
        (Resolution 101 [IV])

Permanent Executive
Committee
(Treaty, Art. 33)

Technical Commission
(Resolution 118 [V])

Secretary
(Treaty, Art. 41)

Consultative
Commission
(Treaty, Art. 43)

International
Accessory
Organizations
ECLA-OAS-IDB
(Treaty, Art. 44)

Accessory Commissions
    Statistics
    Industrial Development
    Origin
    Transport
    Monetary
    Agricultural
    Commercial Policy
    Nomenclature
        (Resolution 41 [II])

System of Zonal Payments
among the Central Banks
Agent:
    Central Bank of Peru
    September 1965

Sectoral Meetings
Machine tools, and special steel
Machines for mining and equipment for the
    petroleum industry
Machines for sewing
Manufactures of industrial transport
    equipment
Manufactures of agricultural machinery
Manufactures of household goods
Electronic and electrical-communication
    industry
Equipment of generation, transmission, and
    distribution of electricity
Producers and users of copper
Fishing industry
Manufactures of fruit and vegetable preserves
Valves for industrial use
Manufactures of abrasives and refractory
    material
Chemical-pharmaceutical industries
Plastic molds
Chemical industry
Contractors of public
    labor
Automotive industry
                            (Resolution 55 [II])

a new mechanism to replace the item-by-item approach to tariff negotiations. A solution to the first problem was attempted with the establishment of the Council of Ministers, and a possible solution to the second problem (that is, automatic tariff reductions) was considered by the Council of Ministers for a decision at their 1967 meeting. At this meeting the relatively less developed countries—Bolivia, Ecuador, and Paraguay—demanded the immediate reduction of tariff barriers in other LAFTA countries, against their goods, arguing that this would help them reach the stage of development of other LAFTA countries. The more developed countries sympathized with the situation of these countries but refused to accept such unilateral and definitive measures.[5]

Action on the following resolutions regarding tariffs was postponed: (1) a resolution calling for an immediate freeze on tariffs and trade restrictions to provide a firm base for future tariff cuts, (2) a resolution suggesting a reorganization of tariffs on items on the Common List to permit a gradual reduction on all by 1973, and (3) a resolution calling for a timetable of tariff advantages for the relatively less developed members of LAFTA.[6] Beyond this no mention was made of plans to begin using automatic tariff reductions to replace the nearly obsolete item-by-item method now in use.

The purpose of a free-trade area is to establish a zone of unrestricted trade among its members. Although it sounds simple, a number of questions have arisen to be faced and solved by LAFTA. For example, there is the question of interpretation of the Treaty regarding the extent to which it is intended to lead toward freeing not only existing trade but also new products not yet traded by the member countries. Most of the trade among LAFTA countries continues to consist of traditional agricultural and mineral products, while the growth of trade in manufactures has been disappointingly slow. In addition, it is becoming increasingly difficult to negotiate the number of concessions required by the National Lists. This happens partly because the easiest concessions have already been made and further concessions are much more difficult, and because negotiating on an item-by-item basis, as discussed earlier, continues to be difficult. Relative to the first problem is a growing complexity of the process of negotiations because of the

[5] *Time,* September 15, 1967, p. 40.

[6] *The New York Times,* September 5, 1967, p. 20.

multiplicity and heterogeneity of duties and restrictions applied to the same product by different countries. Interrelated with this is the extreme complexity of the problem of defining and controlling the origin of products subject to liberalization.

As stated in the Treaty, all trade restrictions on items traded are to be eliminated in 1973. No arrangement has been made, however, to reduce tariffs on products on the Common List before this date, so that the elimination of all tariffs may prove a formidable problem in 1973. Some of the products on the Common List have been placed also on the National List, a tendency increasing in recent years as it becomes difficult to negotiate tariff concessions. To the extent that this duplication continues the problem in 1973 will be reduced.

Achievement of the 1973 deadline for some agricultural products has already been hindered by bottlenecks. Article 23 of the Treaty, which allows special treatment for certain products, has been modified by Resolution 97 (IV) of the Conference.[7] This resolution permits special treatment for agricultural products so that restrictions or tariffs on these products may be continued beyond 1973. This is not surprising, since most of the tariff concessions have been in the manufacturing area, where chemicals and machinery account for almost one half of all negotiations not in the area of agriculture.

Other major bottlenecks encountered by LAFTA are the restricted use of complementarity agreements and the interpretation of the principle of reciprocity. The absence of an agreed program of joint development among the member countries has also been a major factor in slowing down the process of tariff cutting within LAFTA. Differences in the margins of preference offered by various countries and, consequently, in the commercial stimulus provided by the liberalization of the same category of products, have also caused delays. Related to these factors—to some extent resulting from them—is the fact that not all countries have shared equally in the gain brought about by intraregional trade, the larger countries having gained more. The smaller and less developed LAFTA countries have not been inclined to allow the location of new industries to be determined entirely by market forces operating in an environment of regional free trade. They fear that all new industries catering to the regional market will gravitate to the established centers in Argentina, Brazil, or Mexico and that other

[7] LAFTA (Conferencia), *Resoluciones*, 1966, pp. 67–68.

LAFTA countries will gain little or nothing from the process and, indeed, may even lose through the destruction of their existing industries by more powerful competition.

This complication has been recognized; consequently, the Conference in Resolution 75 (III)[8] and Resolution 100 (IV),[9] made it clear that a balanced or equitable amount of development was desired among all countries and not merely the formation of a free-trade area. With the passing of these resolutions LAFTA turned its attention toward the long-run goal of a common market, with a free-trade area representing the first step along the way.

[8] LAFTA (Conferencia), *Resoluciones*, 1966, pp. 16–19.
[9] *Ibid.*, pp. 77–98.

INTEGRATION AND INDUSTRIAL DEVELOPMENT

Besides the reduction of intrazonal tariffs and restrictions to promote integration of LAFTA countries, two other integrating forces are also at work—several subregional integration movements, and strong efforts to integrate by sectors, through complementation agreements.

Subregional Integration

In Bogotá in 1964 the Conference of Contracting Parties of LAFTA first recognized the possibility of organizing subregional agreements as a temporary measure to encourage the overall integration of Latin America. Several subregional integration movements are now underway. For instance, the CACM countries—Costa Rica, El Salvador, Guatemala, Honduras, and Nicaragua—comprise such a subregion; and, more recently, a further subregional movement has taken hold: the so-called Andean Group—Bolivia, Chile, Colombia, Ecuador, Peru, and Venezuela.[1] The agreement among the countries of the River Plata Basin—Argentina, Brazil, Paraguay, and Uruguay—to promote the development of their border areas is another similar attempt at subregional integration.

The growth of the Andean Group is related to dissatisfaction with the structure and mechanism of LAFTA and its Treaty. LAFTA's prob-

---

[1] The Andean Subregional Group, in process of formation over several years, was joined most recently, during 1967, by Bolivia. Formed in anticipation of compliance within the framework of LAFTA's overall rules, the Andean Group has not as yet, by mid-1968, acquired legal status under LAFTA; still pending was the requisite action by LAFTA in agreeing on the compatibility of the Andean Group's statutes with the Treaty of Montevideo. While thus continuing short of formal endorsement under LAFTA, the Andean Group nonetheless proceeded with the formation of organizational structures of its own. Most important, the Andean Development Corporation (ADC) was introduced; patterned along lines of the Chilean Development Corporation, the role envisaged for ADC related to the financing of preinvestment and investment needs within the area, in essence providing the member countries with their counterpart of the CACM area's Central American Bank for Economic Integration.

lems in this respect stem primarily from the fact that the countries of LAFTA are economically too diverse to be united immediately. If the Andean Group countries act separately in the Latin American integration movement the pressure of the market stimulates the industrialization of the three large and more developed economies of Argentina, Brazil, and Mexico. If countries integrate, the size of the market will be more stimulating to industrialization of the countries involved.

Factors favoring integration of the Andean Group countries are their geographical nearness, similar histories, comparable economies, and related cultural backgrounds. The type of economic integration proposed for this group includes the free movement of persons, products, and capital, a common external tariff, and steps advancing the coordination of all economic policies. The Andean Group has officially met several times since 1964 and has worked out an integration plan which includes agreements for joint development of the petrochemical industry, integration of the automobile industry, and joint development of the machinery industry. The plan calls for an immediate 50-percent reduction in tariffs followed by 10-percent reductions each year so that free trade will be established in a period of not more than five years.

The Andean Group looks forward to the following benefits as a result of subregional integration: (1) less vulnerability to foreign fluctuations, (2) better position for discussing international agreements, and (3) more options for advancing a rational industrial policy. In its present relation to LAFTA, the Andean Group has appeared somewhat controversial in that the less developed nations—led by Chile and Colombia—want integration to move as quickly as possible, while the more developed countries—led by Argentina and Brazil—have favored a cautious and careful approach to economic integration, thus guarding against disrupting their economies.[2] Never was the rift between the relatively developed and relatively less developed countries in Latin America more clearly shown than at the recent LAFTA Council of Ministers' meeting when the two groups clashed head on. As a result of this clash the subregional "fourth

[2] For example see the editorial in the *Buenos Aires Herald,* August 10, 1967, as compared with Eduardo Frei, "Integración de America Latina," *Progreso 66/67.*

31

power" group (the Andean Group)[3] was recognized officially by the LAFTA organization.[4]

Sector Integration and Complementation Agreement

The general line of integration followed in LAFTA is similar to that followed by the European Coal and Steel Community—that is, integration by sectors. Presently three main sectors have been established—iron and steel, petrochemicals, and paper and cellulose. Only the first two of these sectors appear to be advancing toward integration throughout LAFTA. Studies for both have been prepared. They contain outlines for complementation agreements, as well as proposals to establish common external tariffs together with internal margins of preference.[5] It is believed by many LAFTA observers that integration by sectors will serve as a strong stepping stone for the eventual creation of a common market.

One step removed from integration by sectors is the complementation agreement. Through the use of complementation agreements two or more member countries can immediately establish free trade and a common external tariff for a specific product or group of products. Access to an enlarged market for manufactures of certain products can facilitate the area-wide development of certain industrial sectors and thus hasten economic integration. The criteria for the creation of a complementation agreement, which can be established on the initiative of either private business or government, are to convince the respective governments that it would achieve these ends: (1) promote industrialization, (2) increase intra-LAFTA trade, and (3) lessen the area's de-

[3] The term "fourth power" was used by LAFTA's Executive Secretary, Gustavo Magarinos, to describe this group as opposed to the other three major Latin American powers—Argentina, Brazil, and Mexico.

[4] Support for subregional integration of the Andean Group or River Plata type has come from the director and president of the Instituto para la Integración de América Latina (INTAL).

[5] W. V. Turnage, LAFTA 1966 in Review. For a complete report see LAFTA (Comisión Asesara de Desarrollo Industrial), Informe de la Secretaria sobre las Resultados del Grupo de Estudio de la Industria Siderurgica, ALALC/CADI/III/dt. 4, September 2, 1966; and Informe de la Secretaria sobre los Resultados del Grupo de Estudio sobre las Industrias Quimicas Derivadas del Petroleo, ALALC/CADI/III/dt. 6, October 7, 1966.

pendence on imports.[6] Complementation industries can be of several types. First, plants in several member countries can manufacture in the same industrial line different products which are then freely traded among participating countries. Second, various components produced in different countries can be traded freely and assembled in some or all of the countries. Third, various production steps can be divided among several countries, after which the goods may be shipped to another country for further processing or final assembly, and then traded freely among the members.[7]

By 1966 four complementation agreements were in existence: statistical machines (Argentina, Brazil, Chile, and Uruguay), 1962; electronic tubes (Argentina, Brazil, Mexico, and Uruguay), 1964; household electrical applicances (Brazil and Uruguay), 1966; electrical communication equipment (Brazil and Uruguay), 1966. The first two agreements have been very successful in terms of increased zonal exports for all countries involved in the agreement. At the Extraordinary Conference meeting in mid-June 1967, Chile, Colombia, Peru, and Uruguay officially presented to the Secretariat a proposal for a complementation agreement covering electrical appliances and components. Early in 1967 all the member countries of LAFTA except Mexico, Bolivia, and Paraguay constructed some form of complementation agreement for the automobile industry. Of special significance was the fact that Chile, Colombia, and Venezuela committed themselves to a duty-free interchange of automobile parts and components. Also important for integration was the fact that Argentina and Brazil, with adequate domestic markets, reached an automobile agreement.

The reason for so few complementation agreements lies in several technical problems related to their operation as well as the massive task of organizing them. It is also reported that the large countries—Argentina, Mexico, and Brazil—see little advantage in a complementation agreement over National Lists and prefer the latter.[8] Complementation agreements recently received support from the Declaration of Presidents, which called for measures "to promote the conclusion

[6] Machinery and Allied Products Institute, *The Latin American Free Trade Association: Progress and Prospects*, May 11, 1967, p. 12.

[7] *Ibid.*, p. 11.

[8] W. V. Turnage, LAFTA *Notes*.

33

of sectoral agreements for industrial complementation, endeavoring to obtain the participation of the countries of relatively less economic development."[9]

Integration by sector (or complementation agreements) is another method that can overcome the problem of economic diversity between countries and the desire for balanced development. These arrangements, covering one product or a group of products, guarantee advantages to the participating countries. The relatively less developed country, in negotiating such agreements, is able to obtain for itself a share of the benefits of integration. Although problems related to the foregoing had a devastating effect on the recent Council of Ministers' meeting, it would appear that solutions are possible through subregional integration efforts and sector integration or complementation agreements.

Industrial Development

LAFTA has three objectives relative to industrial development: (1) to promote more industrial development throughout the area—both import substituting and export creating, (2) to make all industries more efficient through the establishment of a regional market in addition to the national market, and (3) to encourage a balanced economic development among all LAFTA countries, paying special attention to the problems of the relatively less developed countries and the countries considered to have insufficient markets.

The foundations for this policy are found in Resolution 75 (III), which was later expanded in Resolution 100 (IV), both of the Conference, and finally a definite plan of action was established in Resolution 98 of the Committee.[10] The calendar of tasks to be completed by the Accessory Commission on Industrial Development is presented in Figure 2.

The results of the recent meeting show the progress being made by the Accessory Commission on Industrial Development.[11] It was generally agreed that the pace of work should be quickened and that the delegates should concentrate on projects already in progress, rather

[9] *U. S. Department of State Bulletin,* May 8, 1967, p. 714.
[10] LAFTA (Cómite Ejecutivo Permanente), *Resoluciones,* pp. 255–274.
[11] LAFTA (Comisión Asesora de Desarrollo Industrial), *Informe Final de la Tercera Reunión de la Comisión Asesora de Desarrollo Industrial,* ALALC/CADI/III/Informe.

Figure 2. CALENDAR OF TASKS TO BE COMPLETED ON DATE INDICATED BY THE ACCESSORY COMMISSION ON INDUSTRIAL DEVELOPMENT

Month	3rd meeting—1967	4th meeting—1967	5th meeting—1968
June	Examination of a concrete formula of integration planned by the group of study in the steel and petrochemical sectors. Determination of the industrial activities that present possibilities of complementation throughout the area of integration. Identification of possible industries that might be installed in the region to supply the zones demand. A study of the possible forms of complementation in the field of industrial production.		
Sept.		Examination of the specific formulas of integration plans by the group studying in the paper and cellulose industry. Complete studies concerning the establishment of a) the stimulus that can be applied to countries that have installed industry of zonal character, b) the stimulus that can be granted to other countries before the installation of industries of zonal character.	Examination of specific integration plans for the chemical sector.
Dec.	Construction of a new study group with the object of intensifying the work of sector integration. These groups will intensify the work of laying out the integration of different sectors of a zonal type. The work is to be completed by September 1968.		
Tasks of permanent execution.	Confrontation of the national policies of economic development by the Contracting Parties with a view to satisfying the integration objectives. Study the establishment of norms employed to: a) obtain an equitable distribution of industrial integration, b) assure equitable conditions of competition.		

Source: LAFTA (Cómite Ejecutivo Permanente), *Resoluciones* (Montevideo: 1966), pp. 263–266.

35

than diffusing efforts by taking on additional projects. The delegates recommended an increase in the authority of LAFTA regarding integrated industrial-development planning. Specifically, LAFTA should be permitted to set the priorities to be followed by the Inter-American Development Bank (IDB) regarding the financing of multinational studies from the Preinvestment Fund. It was also recommended that the IDB finance the studies carried out by LAFTA. Finally, it was suggested that LAFTA be given a larger role in studies carried out by international agencies, such as ECLA. These measures again indicate the desire of LAFTA members to control their own destinies.[12] Renewed emphasis was placed on the recommendation that IDB immediately initiate preinvestment studies for the location of industry in the relatively less developed countries.[13]

[12] Business International, "Laftagram," *Business Latin America*, July 20, 1967.

[13] Regarding the attitude toward foreign firms, Dr. Raul Prebisch, at a meeting of Mexican industrialists and financiers, supported the "Latinization" of corporate capital. He expressed the desire of restricting new foreign investment to a minority position and in general of permitting it only when foreign technology is required.

ZONAL PAYMENTS SYSTEM

One of the most important factors for the development of a LACM is the establishment and successful operation of an integrated multilateral system of settling accounts between the member countries. Trade throughout Latin America is generally carried on in U.S. dollars, directly or indirectly. So long as countries have to be paid in dollars for their products LAFTA's development will be slowed, and the area's chronic lack of dollars will remain as a major bottleneck hindering intra-LAFTA trade. For this reason financial integration would serve as an effective means for increasing trade and transactions.

The timetable of action for the Accessory Commission on Monetary Affairs, given in Resolution 98 of the Permanent Executive Committee, includes the following items of work to be completed by the end of 1967. First is the perfecting and widening of the credit system for financing intrazonal trade, which implies an intensification of communication among the commercial banks. Second, reports will be prepared concerning the influence that various types of exchange have on ordinary intrazonal trade, on the effects on imports from third countries, and on the treatment applicable to foreign capital. Third, the situation of payments and compensations will be examined, with attention to the forms of cooperation possible between the contracting parties for utilizing domestic and foreign resources to promote integration.

Many of these studies have already been completed, and a system of multilateral compensation is being developed in LAFTA following the framework of bilateral agreements already in existence between Latin American Central Banks. In México in 1965, during the second meeting of the Council on Monetary and Financial policies, an agreement was adopted by the member countries of LAFTA to build on this bilateral framework. This agreement consisted of a simple mechanism of multilateral compensation and reciprocal credits in convertible currencies to settle accounts.[1] The central banks of the member coun-

---

[1] LAFTA, *Sintesis Mensual*, December 1965, pp. 13–17 and 42–46.

tries agreed to use U.S. dollars as the currency for clearing accounts. They consented to establish ordinary lines of reciprocal noninterest-bearing credit which would be processed through bilateral agreements, with accounts settled via cable transfers every two months. It was agreed that no arrangement should interfere with the practice of payments and transfers that exists in each country of the zone.

The Central Bank of Peru has been designated to serve as Agent Bank for the multilateral transfers among the other central banks of LAFTA. The objective of multilateral compensation is to reduce to a minimum the number of transfers between central banks. Forty-eight hours following the last day of every other month, beginning in February, each central bank reports by cable to the Agent Bank the total of the debts that corresponds to payments effectively carried out and registered. The Central Bank of Peru then determines the net balance for each bank and cables within the next twenty-four hours to have the net debits and credits transferred to the respective accounts with the Federal Reserve Bank of New York—designated the common corresponding bank for all central banks.

As of July 1967 fifteen bilateral subagreements provided about $25 million in funds for multilateral transfers.[2] This system is under continuous periodic examination and revision in order to facilitate multilateral operations. Recently the Accessory Commission on Monetary Affairs prepared a new model of technical banking procedures that permits the commercial banks to carry out their operations directly. Arrangements have been made also at the sixth-period sessions of the Conference for authorizing non-LAFTA members to participate in the system of compensation.

A brief progress report on the multilateralization of the bilateral agreements, since the first multilateral compensation in 1966, shows that transfers effectively carried out (up to and including the second two-month compensation) average out to 30 percent of the total amount of the operations over the whole period and for almost every individual compensation. Table 3 shows the multilateral compensations corresponding to the second period of negotiations in 1967. It is seen that in U.S. dollar value a majority (84 percent) of the transfers are carried out between three countries—Argentina, Chile, and Peru—

[2] *Ibid.*, July 1967, pp. 355–359.

TABLE 3

MULTILATERAL COMPENSATION UNDER LAFTA
(Net balances of respective central banks, in thousands of $U.S.)

	Debts		Credits	
	Total	Percent	Total	Percent
Argentina	. . . . .	. .	15,955	83
Mexico	. . . . .	. .	2,886	15
Chile	10,085	53	. . . . .	. .
Colombia	. . . . .	. .	319	2
Peru	8,304	43	. . . . .	. .
Ecuador	718	4	. . . . .	. .
Paraguay	53	. .	. . . . .	. .

Data are up to second period of negotiations, 1967. Data in the cited source, re-arranged and simplified, yield the following additional information (in millions of $U.S.):

		Creditors			
		Argentina	Mexico	Peru	Total
Debtors	Chile	6	2	1	9
	Peru	9	. .	. .	9
	Total	15	2	1	18

Source: LAFTA, *Sintesis Mensual* (Montevideo: July 1967), pp. 355–359.

with Argentina and Peru alone accounting for 50 percent of the transfers. In light of this situation it is interesting to note that by April 30, 1967, the agreements of reciprocal credit between the Central Banks of Argentina and the Central Banks of Chile and Peru were only $5 million. Negotiations are underway, however, to increase this amount.

The developments so far have had positive effects on industry, since delays in receiving payments for LAFTA export sales have decreased. Exporting firms are paid locally when the goods are delivered and the shipping documents are turned over to their private banks. The commercial banks in the member countries collect, in turn, from the central bank, which debits the importing countries' credit line with a settlement of the account every other month.[3]

[3] Business International, LAFTA: *Key to Latin America's 200 Million Consumers.* See chapter on "Financial Roadblocks."

In the event that not every country in the common-market area elects to move toward convertibility, and in the event that distinct trade reorientation occurs for particular countries in consequence of regional integration,[4] the question arises as to how trade imbalances are to be financed. A possibility exists in creation of a payments-clearing system within the region. This, in turn, raises questions of financing. Some outside source of "buffer" foreign exchange probably needs to be considered in order to establish a payments-clearing system. Possible sources include the International Monetary Fund (IMF) and the IDB.[5]

[4] Safeguards are necessary against the possibility that some member country will seek to use a trade imbalance with another member country as an indirect means of securing convertibility for some portion of its normal third-country trade outside the region. Significantly, if no "buffer" of foreign exchange is provided, adjustment in accounts may prove to be harmful via trade contraction (even while the hope is that regional integration may yield trade expansion).

[5] Walter Krause, *The Impact of Latin American Common Markets on the Economies of Member States of the Organization of American States.* For a more detailed discussion see LAFTA (Comisión Asesora de Asuntos Monetarios), *Financiamiento del Balance de Pagos y la Ampliación del Credito Comercial,* ALALC/CAM/V/di 2/Rev. 1, December 12, 1967.

COMMON EXTERNAL TARIFF

The establishment of a common external tariff is the most important step toward a LACM. Because of several unique problems in Latin America, this will be a formidable task for LAFTA. The uniqueness results primarily from the vastly uneven levels of tariffs throughout the area and from the many different types of import restrictions already in existence by the member countries.[1] Countries at different levels of development have varying needs for a common external tariff—relatively more developed countries desiring a lower level of protection than the less developed countries, who prefer a high degree of infant-industry protection. For example, Mexico presently has a lower tariff on machinery than other LAFTA countries and, for this reason, refuses to support the rapid establishment of a common external tariff, which would probably result in higher duties on machinery imports.

Determination of Fair Level of Common Protection

Because LAFTA favors balanced economic development of the member countries, it seems that the final outcome will be biased, to some extent, in favor of the relatively less developed countries. How to make this consistent with the Council of Ministers' meeting in 1966, which called for "the establishment of a common external tariff at levels that will provide efficiency and productivity," will have to be given serious thought.

[1] A general statement concerning tariffs and restrictions for LAFTA countries would say nothing more than that they are variable in each country and between countries. Space prohibits any accurate representation of actual tariffs and restrictions. For persons interested, a good summary is presented by Business International, *Business Latin America*, July 6 and 13, 1967; a detailed explanation is available in LAFTA (Cómite Ejecutivo Permanente), *Restricciones Aplicables a la Importación de Mercaderías, Vigentes en los Paises de la* ALALC, CEP/Repartido 820/Rev. 1, June 13, 1967, and *Derechos Aduaneros y Gravamenes de Efectos Equivalentes Aplicables a la Importación de Mercaderías, Vigentes en los Paises de la* ALALC, CEP/Repartido 819/Rev. 1, June 14, 1967.

The main purpose of a common external tariff usually is to provide a protective barrier around the region to encourage more intraregional trade. In the case of developing countries, however, other considerations must be taken into account. First, it is important that the cost of imports required for national and regional economic development be kept low. Second, a necessary, but difficult, task (because of the economic diversity of the countries) is to coordinate the common external tariff with development plans of individual countries. Third, in determining the level of the common external tariff it is most important in LAFTA's relation with outside countries that there be trade-creating effects so that member countries can earn foreign exchange in order both to finance more industrialization and to pay rapidly rising debt-service costs. Moreover, the level of protection must be sufficiently high so that intra-LAFTA trade can replace imports or serve as an add-on to existing trade. For no reason, however, should the level of protection be allowed to threaten the rate of growth of exports to outside countries.

Another problem, that will be pressing in the near future, is the statement of a position taken in regard to the General Agreement on Tariffs and Trade (GATT). Brazil, Chile, Peru, and Uruguay, as members of GATT, are obliged to extend to other members of that organization any concession granted to another country. Under this provision the advantages of LAFTA would disappear because the preferential treatment it secures for its members must also be extended to other GATT countries. However, Article 24 of GATT exempts from this obligation the contracting parties of a customs union or free-trade area. GATT stipulates in Paragraph 5 of Article 24 that the external duties of a customs union must not be higher or more restrictive than the corresponding duties and other restrictions in force among the member nations prior to the formation of such a union and that all trade barriers between the member nations must be eliminated. The developing countries of Latin America, however, criticize GATT because its procedure confines the benefits of trade liberalization to the initially high-tariff countries or the developed countries. The GATT liberalization procedure requires the existence of protective policies to enable a country to bargain for trade liberalization.[2]

[2] For a more extensive treatment see Harry G. Johnson, *The World Economy at the Crossroads*, pp. 42–49.

It is possible that the drive to develop specific industries may gain momentum with a higher common external tariff. There is little doubt that should LAFTA's interests conflict with those of GATT, the member countries will give up their membership in GATT. Mexico has provided Latin American countries with a good example of how to benefit from all GATT trade agreements (because of its trade with the United States, which grants reciprocal treatment to all countries) while at the same time controlling the concessions it grants other nations.

There are some problems in establishing the right level of protection for all countries. First, some protection differences among various countries will always exist, because of transport costs. For example, the cost of shipping between the United States and Mexico is lower than that between the United States and Argentina. Second, defining efficiency is a difficult task in a developing country, because of the lack of adequate complementary factors of production, such as skilled labor, energy, and subsidiary and complementary industries. Third, since a common external tariff is designed to encourage and protect the growth of domestic or regional industries producing capital goods, it results in high costs for basic industries which are needed most but has no similar effect on other industries.

Major Resolutions

The Treaty of Montevideo, in 1960, instituted the formation of a common external tariff and set in motion the eventual trend toward a common market. In Article 15 the Contracting Parties agreed to make every effort, in keeping with the liberalization objectives of the Treaty, to reconcile their import and export regimes, as well as the treatment they accord to foreign capital. Article 24 stated that countries should make all efforts to establish a common market and that LAFTA should undertake studies to consider projects and plans to achieve this purpose with the help of international organizations.

The next important legislation came in Resolution 75 (III) of the Conference, designed to coordinate economic and commercial policies and to harmonize the system of foreign-trade control, necessary because the countries of LAFTA have great diversity in their treatment of imports from third countries. This diversity, which gives rise to a growing complexity in the negotiation process, is portrayed by the multiplicity and heterogeneity of duties and restrictions applied to the same product in different countries, and by differences in the margin of preference and, consequently, in the commercial stimulus provided in the various countries by the liberalization of the same category of products. The fulfillment of Resolution 75 (III) is further hindered by the difficulty in the application and interpretation of the principle of reciprocity laid down in the Treaty, distortions of normal conditions of competition between regional producers, difficulties from differences in the cost of inputs imported from outside the region which may affect the location of new investments, and the complexity of defining and controlling the regional origin of products subject to liberalization.

Balanced economic and social development, as stipulated by the Treaty, requires harmonizing economic and commercial policies. The initial research along these lines began in 1964; in 1966 an advisory committee on customs affairs directed attention toward a revision of NABALALC (the tariff nomenclature of Brussels as used and modified by LAFTA) for adoption as the common-market nomenclature, and a study of the customs duties and restrictions applied to imports of each product in the various countries. The reasoning was that the establishment of a common external tariff required the conversion of these customs duties and restrictions into ad-valorem terms based on the c.i.f. value of products which would then be categorized under NABALALC classification.

As a result of these studies the Fourth Conference of Contracting Parties, in 1964, adopted Resolution 100 (IV), which is directed toward reaching the objectives of Article 54 of the Treaty and establishes a program of action for Resolution 75 (III). In specifying the action plan it was emphasized that care should be taken to obtain an equitable distribution of the results of the process of integration and to assure equitable conditions of competition. Both of these conditions are especially relevant to the relatively less developed countries.

Although the program of action is specified for all sectors of the economy affected by economic integration, concentration is on the basic directives and plan of action for customs affairs. In this respect the main goal is to establish a common external tariff that will not present distortion among the contracting parties. It was also stated that the program of harmonization of the instruments regulating foreign trade should be tied to the progressive elimination of the barriers to intrazonal trade, while maintaining equitable conditions of competition to facilitate the completion of the liberalization program. In addition, the common external tariff should take into account the stimulation of economic activity throughout the zone, avoiding the inefficient production of goods resulting from exaggerated protection, yet establishing an effective protective barrier in favor of zonal production and a defense against possible excessive external competition. Also considered was the desirability of proceeding with the gradual establishment of a common external tariff for certain economic sectors or groups of products.

Following these basic directives, late in 1966 the Permanent Executive Committee passed Resolution 98, which established a calendar for the completion of tasks and studies of the program of action of Resolution 100 (IV). This calendar of tasks, to be carried out by the Accessory Commission on Trade Policy, is presented in Figure 3. Let us examine the progress made toward completion of these tasks.

Recent Developments in Trade Policy

One month after passing Resolution 98 the Permanent Executive Committee, through Resolution 104,[3] created a special group to study the implementation of the common external tariff in view of Resolution 100 (IV) and Resolution 98. In December 1966 the Council of Ministers reiterated, through Resolution 170,[4] the need to establish a common external tariff. This resolution stated that to obtain harmonization in the treatment extended to third countries, the Contracting Parties need to cooperate toward achieving a more accelerated process of reducing tariffs. It further emphasized the need to consider establishing different speeds of external tariff adjustment in the cases of the relatively less developed and insufficient-market countries. Special consideration should be given also to agricultural products. Elements of flexibility (within the general framework of the Treaty) should be introduced to permit adjustment between aims and their applied effects in terms of quantity and structure. Furthermore, the resolution emphasized the need to coordinate the program of freeing intrazonal

---

[3] LAFTA (Cómite Ejecutivo Permanente), *Resolución 104*, October 20, 1966. For additional background material see LAFTA, *Sintesis Mensual*, October 1965, pp. 17–26.
[4] LAFTA (Council of Ministers), *Resolución 170* (CM-I/II-E).

Figure 3. CALENDAR OF TASKS TO BE COMPLETED ON DATE INDICATED BY THE ACCESSORY COMMISSION ON TRADE POLICY AS ESTABLISHED IN RESOLUTION 98 OF THE COMMITTEE

End of Month	1966	1967	1968	1969	1970
March		Presentation of schedules comparing the levels of tariffs and restrictions.			
June			Standardization and unification of customs documents used in the operation of foreign trade. Once completed and approved by the governments of the Contracting Parties, it will be incorporated into the code of uniform customs laws. Consideration of the common definition of customs terms and the necessary methodology for the establishment of a glossary of terms of Latin American customs.		
Sept.	Delivery of the plans of tariffs and restrictions applicable to third countries corresponding to 99 chapters of NABALALC.	Presentation of the nomenclature pertaining to a uniform tariff by the Secretary to the Permanent Executive Committee. Projects of common norms or other special customs requirements (customs transit of merchandise and temporary admission of vehicles that transport merchandise) to be included in the uniform code of customs law.			
Dec.	Projects of the common norms used in the regular admission of trade patterns. Outline of the material that will be included in the uniform code of customs law and methodology of work to be elaborated.	Study of the imposed internal discrimination that reigns over merchandise imports. Project of common norms used as regular rules for the promotion of exports such as temporary admission drawback, and replacement of primary material without payment of tariff.	The Secretary will elaborate upon a study in which there will be an examination of problems and progress of harmonization of the regulatory investments of foreign trade and plan a base of the common trade policy of the Contracting Parties. Besides the basic directives of economic policy established in Resolution 100 the following should be taken into account: a) the results of the comparative anaylsis of tariffs and restrictions that the countries of the zone		

End of Month	1966	1967	1968	1969	1970
Dec.		Establish a minimum program of customs authorization that can be used by the countries of the zone which have not undertaken activities of this nature. This might include initiating schools for customs officers of member countries, providing regular courses to explain the customs authorization of LAFTA.	apply to the imports from third countries, b) conclusions or recommendations formulated by the organs of the Association on matters of harmonization of the instruments regulating foreign trade, c) the criteria recommended by the technical organs of the Association on matters of economic policy and foreign trade, and d) the experience gained in the examination of the results reached in intrazonal trade through the program of liberalization.		
		Preparation of a program for the establishment of a group of studies that will contain the directives, instructions, and corresponding methodology for the elaboration of the steps of the program of a common external tariff. This group will take into account the following basic principles: a) include as large a number as possible of the tariffs and restrictions applied to the imports from third countries with the object of avoiding distortions that could provoke differences in existing treatment, b) create conditions that permit the establishment of a common market in agreement with Article 54 of the Treaty, c) obtain fair conditions of competition that facilitate the fulfillment of the program of liberalization, d) provide the Contracting Parties the additional disposition to face the particular problems of each country in its trade with third countries, and e) examine the possibility and convenience of proceeding with a gradual harmonization by sectors of production or groups of products giving priority to those that will be of greater importance for economic development of the region. Elaboration of a uniform customs code of laws taking into account the above-mentioned studies.			

Source: LAFTA, Cómite Ejecutivo Permanente, *Resoluciones* (Montevideo: 1966), pp. 255–262.

trade through the mechanism of automatic tariff reduction with the gradual establishment of a common external tariff.

Meanwhile, Resolution 122 (V)[5] of the Conference officially endorsed an ad-valorem system of tariff evaluation with provisions for official values and specific rates, when necessary, as the base for the establishment of common customs instruments and mechanisms corresponding to the harmonization of treatment to third countries. Resolution 133 (V)[6] of the Conference adopted the system of notation of Brussels to identify products for the purpose of establishing zonal tariffs. LAFTA is currently attempting to convert duties and charges on imported goods to a single ad-valorem percentage of the free-market price of each product. However, it is likely to take some time before all the members will complete this reform of their tariff systems.[7]

The Study Group on the Common External Tariff

The first meeting of the study group on the common external tariff, from April 24 to May 12, 1967, was attended by all the countries of LAFTA except Colombia and Bolivia. At this meeting the Secretary presented his opinions regarding some of the objectives, problems, and considerations that should be studied in closer detail.[8] He emphasized three objectives directly related to integration which should be carefully examined in the development of the common external tariff: (1) assurance of equitable conditions of competition throughout the zone for all national markets, (2) establishment of reasonable and sufficient protection to encourage the individual development of the region maintaining the highest efficiency possible, and (3) endowment of LAFTA with the instruments to negotiate as a unified block. Other factors that should be given attention are the balance-of-payments effect and related adjustments, the need to accumulate foreign exchange for development purposes, employment-creating possibilities, and redistribution of income to effect a modification of the role of the agricultural sector.

[5] LAFTA (Conferencia), *Resoluciones*, 1966, pp. 125–127.
[6] *Ibid.*, pp. 135–139.
[7] Business International, LAFTA: *Key to Latin America's 200 Million Consumers*.
[8] LAFTA, Working Paper, CEP/GE. AEC/I/J, May 3, 1967.

The Secretary offered several positive suggestions for the common external tariff: (1) the establishment of a bargaining tariff at a higher level than appropriate (in all or certain categories of goods) in order to have margins of reduction negotiated with third countries, a procedure which may involve problems, because when not negotiated it creates abnormal conditions providing excessive protection; (2) a maximum tariff applicable to the countries or groups of nations which have not arranged preferential trade agreements, and a minimum tariff that would govern for preferential treatment, a procedure which, though discriminatory, represents a considerable fortification of the negotiated position of countries; (3) consideration of the possibility of initiating mechanisms of trade restoration through the application of imposed compensation or other mechanisms in order to discourage measures opposed to regional interests.

The report of this first meeting of the study group on the common external tariff set forth the economic goals of the common external tariff and reiterated the points emphasized in the Secretary's report. The study group stressed the need for flexibility to permit adjustments to the special problems of the less developed countries. It was admitted as a basic criterion that the instruments of the common external tariff should embrace all products but, in an intermediate period, may apply to only some areas. Nevertheless, the program of harmonization of the regulatory instruments of foreign trade should be directly tied to the progressive elimination of the barriers to intrazonal trade. The study group also assigned special importance to determining the methodology that should be used in the calculation and establishment of the common external tariff. The following classifications of products were considered as the basis for determining the range of the common external tariff: (1) economic categories of products—for example, raw materials, intermediate products, and final products; (2) industrial sectors or groups of products; (3) chapters or groups of similar chapters of NABALALC; and (4) some combination of these classes. The group did not decide on one methodology but recommended that (1) and (2) be more fully investigated.

The group also considered the problems of the procedure for the application of the common external tariff. They suggested that its establishment should take fifteen years, at most, through a series of progressive steps integrated with the program of intraregional tariff reduction. After each step is completed the results will be analyzed and pertinent measures adopted to facilitate the completion of the program.

The private sector also will take part in the formation of the common external tariff. The study group will request cost and production data from the private sector. Investment plans also will be considered to assure adequate protection for industries that will be developed in the near future. Firms will be unable to predict the level of the common external tariff simply by averaging the existing national tariffs. The final level will most likely be established through negotiations, rather than by any mathematical method. Thus, firms cannot assume that any trend in the external tariff system will be maintained.[9]

A most important move toward the establishment of a common external tariff and a LACM was the endorsement contained in the Declaration of the Presidents of America at Punta del Este in April 1967.[10] Of immediate concern to us are the measures regarding LAFTA in Chapter I, Section 2. Here the Presidents of the countries of LAFTA agreed to instruct their respective Ministers of Foreign Affairs participating in the Council of Ministers meeting in 1967 to adopt measures necessary to implement the establishment of a LACM, these efforts to begin in 1970 and to be completed in a period of not more than fifteen years. Within this context emphasis was put on the need to progressively establish a common external tariff, taking into consideration the promotion of efficiency and productivity, harmonized with the programed elimination of tariffs and other restrictions of the member countries.

Other progress toward the establishment of a common external tariff was the completion in June 1967 of two extensive reports on the existing restrictions and tariffs against imports by member countries.[11] These reports indicate a wide variety of tariffs, restrictions, and pro-

[9] Business International, "Building a Common Outer Tariff Raises Complex Issues for LAFTA Study Group," *Business Latin America*, June 1, 1967.

[10] For text see *U.S. Department of State Bulletin*, May 8, 1967, pp. 714–721.

[11] LAFTA (Cómite Ejecutivo Permanente), *Derechos Aduaneros y Gravamenes de Efectos Equivalentes Aplicables a la Importación de Mercaderías, Vigentes en los Paises de la ALALC*, CEP/Repartido, 819/Rev. 1, June 14, 1967, and *Restricciones Aplicables a la Importación de Mercaderías, Vigentes en los Paises de la ALALC*, CEP/Repartido 820/Rev. 1, June 13, 1967.

hibitive procedures against imports which vary considerably from country to country.

In the latter half of 1967 the head of the study group on the common external tariff, Alfredo Blom Flor, indicated that work on the common external tariff was just beginning and, therefore, it was unlikely that much would be decided concerning it at the Council of Ministers meeting in Asunción. Currently the study group is concerned with defining all the tariffs and restrictions that countries impose against imports, establishing and making operational the common norm of classification (NABALALC) and testing possible ad-valorem duties on products, determining the origin of products, and examining the extent to which many tariffs are being replaced by various types of restrictions. The question is how to coordinate them into a common external tariff that would ensure balanced economic development among all countries of LAFTA. Care was also taken to coordinate the common external tariff with industrial development, special attention being given to the particular sectors of integration.[12]

Some LAFTA officials believe the common external tariff, when negotiated by the member countries, will be determined on the basis of specific industries (such as iron, steel, petrochemicals, and paper) or by groups of products. Additionally, attention is directed toward the relative level of development in each country, taking into consideration the goal of balanced development of the member countries.

In the recent Council of Ministers meeting, August 28 to September 2, 1967, in Asunción, the matter of the common external tariff was discussed. Any action on this subject, however, was postponed until the next meeting. Meanwhile the issue has been referred to the Permanent Executive Committee for further study. It was agreed that next year a group within LAFTA—the Andean community—would "abolish

---

[12] Many of these tasks are currently being carried out by the Accessory Commission on Industrial Development. This commission, through compilation of statistics on costs and prices of Latin American firms and comparison of them with those of European and U.S. firms, is undertaking intensive studies to determine the amount of real protection needed by Latin American industries. The Commission is undertaking also a study to determine the various degrees of elaboration or processing of products from raw materials to finished goods. They are considering the possibility of arranging goods of similar degrees of processing in various grade levels with a common external tariff assigned according to each grade.

51

virtually all tariffs and quota restrictions among its members and establish a minimum common external tariff for nations outside the association."[13] The major bottleneck to action at this meeting was the rift between the more developed countries and the less developed countries.

[13] *The New York Times*, September 1, 1967, p. 23.

PART III

IMPLICATIONS FOR THE FUTURE

EVALUATION OF PROGRESS

The success of LAFTA and the outlook for its future can best be perceived by examining the development of intrazonal trade, extrazonal trade, and changes in per capita income and productivity of major sectors prior to and after the signing of the treaty in 1960. Regardless how favorable the results, continued success depends on finding a solution to the basic problems of financing economic integration and the treatment of the relatively less-developed countries. Important, from the standpoint of world attitude toward regional economic integration in Latin America, is the reaction of international business. Another consideration having a significant effect on integration is the United States attitude toward a LACM.

This section will entail a careful analysis of those issues which are basic to the future outlook concerning the eventual establishment of a LACM. The discussion will be approached from the standpoint of the present or future developmental impact resulting from economic integration.

INTRAZONAL TRADE

An important test in determining the successful establishment of a free-trade area is to examine the amount of free trade generated between the member countries. Let us briefly examine some of the highlights of LAFTA's intrazonal trade. Table 4 presents a long-run view of the changing patterns of trade among the member countries. The data show that both exports and imports increased sharply between 1934 and 1951 for all countries. In 1951–1952 this trend reversed itself and a general decrease in exports and imports continued in almost all countries until the signing of the Treaty of Montevideo in 1960. Since 1961 exports and imports of all member countries have increased, approaching or surpassing the 1951–1952 peak. Between 1961 and 1964 intrazonal exports doubled, and until 1965 the annual increase averaged 20 percent or more. The following figure shows the relative increases in LAFTA intrazonal trade between 1961 and 1966. The comparatively slack performance in 1966 resulted primarily from decreased zonal imports of 11 percent for Argentina and of 12 percent for Brazil, which together account for about 60 percent of all LAFTA intrazonal trade. Exports in 1966 declined by 8 percent in Brazil, while they increased by 55 percent in Mexico, and by 75 percent in Colombia and Uruguay. Although the percentage increases are large for the latter three countries, their total absolute gain in exports was a modest $43 million.

Estimated figures for 1967 showed an increase of about 10 percent above the levels reached in the same periods of 1966. The majority of this expansion is accounted for by the phenomenal increase (about 50 percent) in Argentina's exports to the zone. Mexico's exports, however, are failing to increase above 1966 levels and intrazonal exports of Colombia, Peru, and Uruguay also have fallen sharply, while Brazil and Paraguay have experienced modest declines. The increase in Argentina's exports coincides with the devaluation of the Argentine peso early in 1967.

Figures 5 and 6 show the rate of change of intrazonal exports and imports by country. Countries experiencing the greatest rate of change between 1950 and 1966 in exports are Mexico and Colombia, while the export patterns of the remaining countries can be described with an almost horizontal trend line. During the same period, and primarily since the signing of the Treaty, imports of Mexico, Chile, Colombia, Peru, and Ecuador experienced the greatest rates of increase.

A comparison of the percentage change in intrazonal trade between the periods 1946/51–1966 and 1961–1966 (Table 4) shows substantially larger values in the latter period—35 as compared to 126 for exports and 50 as compared to 119 for imports for all LAFTA. During 1961–1966 the most substantial percentage increases in intrazonal exports have been experienced by Mexico (616), Colombia (377), Uruguay (360), and Argentina (142). For intrazonal imports during the same period the countries undergoing the greatest percentage change are Mexico (721), Colombia (449), Brazil (270), and Peru (188). However, a general evaluation leads to the conclusion that since 1965 this rate of increase has been slowing down for most countries. In this year the upward trend for exports increased only 13 percent as compared to 31 percent in 1964, 20 percent in 1963, and 19 percent in 1962. For imports the corresponding percentage increases were 17 in 1965, 23 in 1964, 25 in 1963, and 16 in 1962.[1] Between 1961 and 1964 intrazonal trade increased at the same rate in all the member countries except Mexico, which registered a faster rate. This trend begins to change in 1964–1965. Brazil's intrazonal exports increased by almost 50 percent between 1963 and 1965, acounting for 90 percent of the increase in intrazonal trade during this period. With imports, Mexico, Colombia, and to a lesser extent Argentina, experienced a continued rate of increase. On the basis of this information it can be concluded that LAFTA has been successful in substantially expanding intrazonal trade.

Corresponding with LAFTA's desire to expand intrazonal trade is the emphasis on an equitable distribution of the benefits among all countries so that all will experience development. In this respect Figures 7 and 8 show the percentage distribution of intrazonal trade among countries. Figure 7 shows Argentina and Brazil maintaining a dominant role in intrazonal exports, a trend which does not appear to be changing. While the relative shares of intrazonal exports of Chile

[1] UN, *Economic Survey of Latin America, 1965*, p. 50.

TABLE 4

INTRAZONAL TRADE BY COUNTRY, 1934-1966

(Value in millions of $U.S.)

EXPORTS (f.o.b.)

	1934–1938		1946–1951		1952		1953–1955		1956–1958		1959–1961		1961	
	Value	Percent	Value	Percent	Value	Percent	Value	Percent	Value	Percent	Value	Percent	Value	Percent
Argentina	47.0	41.6	181.8	36.5	93.9	21.4	204.9	40.3	123.4	32.6	133.4	41.6	100.0	33.5
Brazil	21.7	19.4	136.4	27.4	126.2	28.8	132.5	26.4	127.6	33.7	85.6	26.6	95.3	31.9
Mexico	4.8	4.2	28.9	5.8	22.6	5.2	5.2	1.0	5.0	1.5	6.2	1.9	7.9	2.6
Chile	5.9	5.2	45.8	9.3	70.8	16.2	58.7	11.6	36.2	9.6	34.9	10.8	34.8	11.7
Colombia	0.5	.4	5.1	1.0	4.5	1.0	3.0	.6	3.7	1.1	4.5	1.4	6.2	2.0
Peru	12.0	10.6	60.3	12.1	74.1	16.9	50.1	9.9	42.2	11.2	37.2	11.6	31.6	10.6
Uruguay	9.4	8.5	15.3	3.0	30.7	7.1	28.7	5.7	16.7	4.4	3.9	1.4	5.8	1.9
Ecuador	2.9	2.5	12.7	2.6	6.7	1.5	9.8	1.9	8.7	2.3	6.5	2.0	7.5	2.5
Paraguay	8.6	7.6	11.4	2.3	8.5	1.9	13.3	2.6	13.6	3.6	8.7	2.7	9.9	3.3
Total	112.8	100.0	497.7	100.0	438.0	100.0	507.7	100.0	378.2	100.0	321.0	100.0	299.0	100.0

	1962		1963		1964		1965		1966		1946/51–1966 Percentage change	1961–1966 Percentage change
	Value	Percent	Value	Percent	Value	Percent	Value	Percent	Value	Percent		
Argentina	141.4	39.9	185.0	43.5	218.4	39.3	231.1	36.4	242.7	35.9	33	142
Brazil	75.8	21.4	76.0	17.9	132.8	23.9	197.4	31.1	181.5	26.9	33	90
Mexico	16.7	4.7	25.9	6.1	33.9	6.1	36.3	5.7	56.7	8.4	95	616
Chile	39.4	11.1	49.3	11.6	54.5	9.8	53.2	8.4	53.7	7.9	17	54
Colombia	7.3	2.1	6.1	1.4	10.9	1.9	16.7	2.6	29.1	4.3	470	377
Peru	48.8	13.8	49.1	11.6	63.8	11.5	54.1	8.5	52.3	7.7	−13	66
Uruguay	8.0	2.3	15.0	3.5	15.0	2.7	15.6	2.5	26.8	3.9	74	360
Ecuador	6.1	1.7	8.0	1.7	11.1	2.0	13.2	2.1	12.5	1.7	−1	66
Paraguay	10.8	3.0	10.7	2.5	14.8	2.7	17.6	2.8	19.9	2.9	74	101
Total	354.3	100.0	425.2	100.0	555.4	100.0	635.2	100.0	675.2	100.0	35	126

Source: Data years 1934–1952 from UN, *Study of Inter-Latin American Trade* (New York: 1957), pp. 19–22; for years 1953–1961 from UN, *Economic Survey of Latin America, 1965* (New York: 1967), pp. 49–50; for years 1961–1966 from LAFTA (Cómite Ejecutivo Permanente), *Comercio Intrazonal por Paises de Destino Procedencia,* CEP/Repartido 876/Add. (Montevideo: August 14, 1967).

TABLE 4 (Continued)

INTRAZONAL TRADE BY COUNTRY, 1934–1966

IMPORTS (c.i.f.)

	1934–1938		1946–1951		1952		1953–1955		1956–1958		1950–1961		1961	
	Value	Percent	Value	Percent	Value	Percent	Value	Percent	Value	Percent	Value	Percent	Value	Percent
Argentina[a]	37.5	32.5	182.7	34.8	267.4	42.1	185.7	33.0	164.1	39.2	113.3	31.1	126.0	34.9
Brazil	41.5	35.8	137.3	26.3	173.4	27.2	185.9	33.0	112.6	26.9	90.1	24.1	45.2	12.5
Mexico	1.1	.9	10.0	1.9	5.7	.9	1.8	.3	2.8	.6	3.9	1.1	4.1	1.2
Chile	11.4	9.8	72.9	13.9	77.6	12.2	81.3	14.5	54.8	13.2	76.9	21.3	94.5	26.2
Colombia	1.8	1.5	25.9	4.9	16.3	2.6	16.5	2.9	11.0	2.6	8.6	2.4	10.2	2.8
Peru	5.8	5.0	24.6	4.7	19.9	3.1	20.7	3.6	23.6	5.6	26.7	7.3	31.8	8.8
Uruguay	11.0[b]	9.5	55.0	10.4	64.4	10.1	53.1	9.4	34.7	8.3	31.4	8.6	34.5	9.6
Ecuador	0.8[b]	.7	4.3	.8	3.8	.6	5.5	1.0	3.8	.9	3.3	.9	4.1	1.1
Paraguay	4.9	4.2	11.8	2.2	7.7	1.2	11.6	2.3	11.2	2.7	9.6	2.6	9.8	2.7
Total	115..8	100.0	524.5	100.0	636.2	100.0	562.1	100.0	418.6	100.0	363.8	100.0	360.2	100.0

	1962		1963		1964		1965		1966		1946/51–1966	1961–1966
	Value	Percent	Value	Percent	Value	Percent	Value	Percent	Value	Percent	Percentage change	Percentage change
Argentina	103.2	24.6	101.6	19.4	170.7	26.5	255.7	33.1	226.7	28.9	24	79
Brazil	128.6	30.6	163.9	31.2	167.9	26.0	190.4	24.7	167.0	21.3	22	270
Mexico	6.1	1.5	10.8	2.1	17.3	2.7	29.7	3.9	33.7	4.3	237	721
Chile	80.5	19.2	120.0	22.9	128.9	19.9	122.1	15.8	140.9	17.9	94	49
Colombia	12.5	2.9	21.4	4.1	33.1	5.1	38.4	4.9	56.0	7.1	116	449
Peru	45.2	10.8	62.0	11.8	58.9	9.1	80.9	10.5	91.5	11.7	272	188
Uruguay	34.0	8.1	31.8	6.1	49.3	7.6	32.1	4.2	46.0	5.9	−16	33
Ecuador	3.9	0.9	5.2	0.9	7.6	1.2	8.9	1.2	8.3	1.1	93	102
Paraguay	6.0	1.4	8.4	1.6	11.6	1.8	13.3	1.7	14.3	1.8	21	46
Total	420.1	100.0	525.1	100.0	545.3	100.0	771.5	100.0	784.6	100.0	50	119

[a] Value is presented in c. & f.
[b] 1938.

Figure 4

INDEX OF THE EVOLUTION OF INTRAZONAL TRADE OF LAFTA

(1961=100)

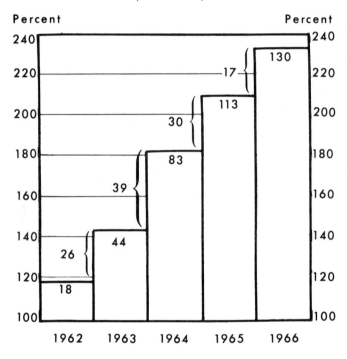

Source: LAFTA, (Cómite Ejecutive Permanente), *ALALC Comercio Intrazonal Primer Quinquento del Tratado de Montevideo, 1962-1966,* CEP/Repartido 787 (Montevideo: March 14, 1967), p. 2.

Figure 5

RATE OF CHANGE AND DISTRIBUTION OF INTRAZONAL EXPORTS
BY COUNTRY, 1948-1966 (F.O.B. VALUE)

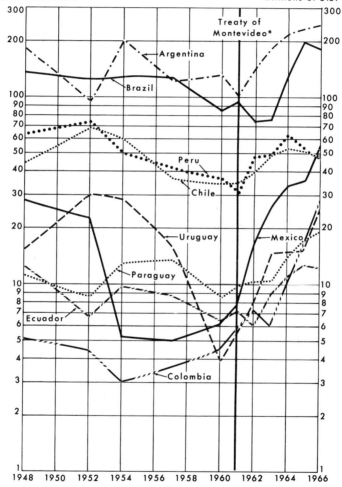

*The Treaty was signed in 1960 and became effective in 1961.
Source: See Table 4.

Figure 6

**RATE OF CHANGE AND DISTRIBUTION OF INTRAZONAL IMPORTS
BY COUNTRY, 1948-1966 (C.I.F. VALUE)**

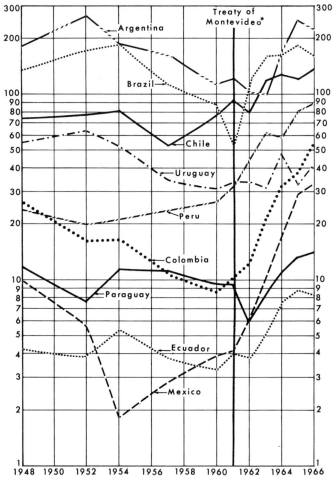

*The Treaty was signed in 1960 and became effective in 1961.

Source: See Table 4.

62

Figure 7

PERCENTAGE DISTRIBUTION OF INTRAREGIONAL EXPORTS (F.O.B.)
BY COUNTRY OF ORIGIN, 1948-1966

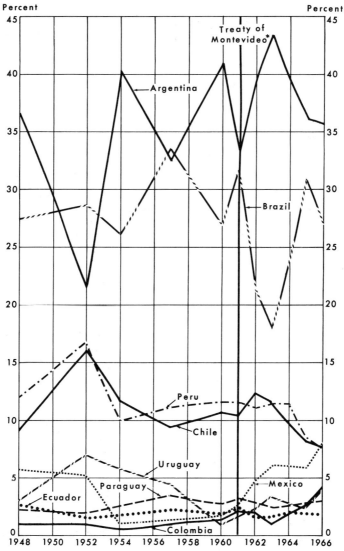

*The Treaty was signed in 1960 and became effective in 1961.
Source: See Table 4.

63

Figure 8

PERCENTAGE DISTRIBUTION OF INTRAREGIONAL IMPORTS (C.I.F.)
BY COUNTRY OF ORIGIN, 1948-1966

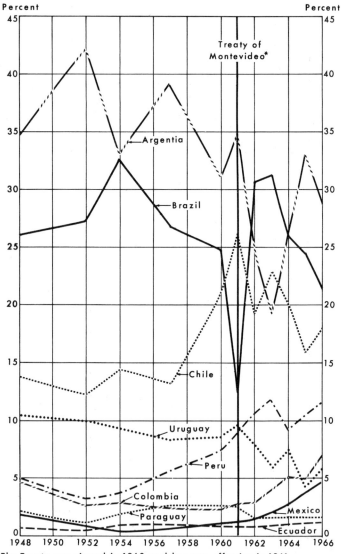

*The Treaty was signed in 1960 and became effective in 1961.
Source: See Table 4.

64

and Peru have decreased, Mexico has enjoyed a substantial increase. In general, the remaining countries have experienced no significant change in their share of intrazonal trade. Presently, Argentina accounts for 35–40 percent of intrazonal trade; Brazil, between 20 and 30 percent; Chile, Mexico, and Peru, from 5 to 12 percent each; while Colombia, Ecuador, Paraguay, and Uruguay account for 2 to 3 percent each.

The situation is slightly different with imports (Figure 8), the overall trend decreasing for Argentina, Brazil, and Uruguay, and to a lesser extent Chile, while increasing for Colombia, Mexico, and Peru. The remaining countries have experienced no appreciable change. Mexico, Colombia, and Ecuador account for 2 to 6 percent while Chile, Uruguay, and Paraguay absorb 20 to 30 percent of total intrazonal imports. In total, Argentina, Brazil, and Chile account for over 75 percent of intrazonal trade; Peru accounts for about 10 percent; Mexico, Colombia, and Uruguay together account for less than 5 percent.

In order to determine the degree to which the formation of LAFTA has resulted in the increase in intrazonal trade it is necessary to examine the relationship between changes in intrazonal trade and tariff concessions granted by each country. Table 5 shows the annual and cumulative tariff concessions granted by each country and what percent each country's concessions represent of the total number of negotiations. As shown by the table, the majority of concessions were granted the first two years of the Treaty. The pattern since that time is summarized in the following table.[2] The major additions to this list were made by Argentina (549), Mexico (423), and Brazil (353).

Conference	Additional concessions	Percent increase
3	655	8.6
4	226	2.7
5	580	6.8
6	339	3.7

Argentina, Brazil, and Ecuador have each granted over 1,600 concessions as of 1966, and together these countries have accounted for more

[2] For a more detailed treatment see W. V. Turnage, LAFTA *Tariff Concessions and Zonal Trade.*

TABLE 5

LAFTA: EVALUATION OF TARIFF CONCESSIONS, 1961–1966

Negotiations

	First round 1961	Percent	Second round 1962	Cum.	Percent	Third round 1963	Cum.	Percent	Fourth round 1964	Cum.	Percent	Fifth round 1965	Cum.	Percent	Sixth round 1966	Cum.	Percent
Argentina	414	12.7	658	1072	14.1	208	1280	15.5	83	1363	16.1	174	1537	17.0	84	1621	17.3
Brazil	619	19.0	631	1250	16.5	62	1312	15.9	40	1352	16.0	159	1511	16.7	92	1603	17.1
Mexico	288	8.9	319	607	8.0	120	727	8.8	75	802	9.5	135	937	10.4	93	1030	11.0
Chile	343	10.6	490	833	11.0	31	864	10.5	8	872	10.3	22	894	9.9	23	917	9.7
Colombia	268	8.3	351	619	8.1	85	704	8.5	10	714	8.4	31	745	8.2	6	751	8.0
Peru	227	7.0	72	299	3.9	56	355	4.3	9	364	4.3	28	392	4.3	10	402	4.3
Uruguay	567	17.5	43	610	8.0	54	664	8.1	0	664	7.8	12	676	7.4	13	689	7.3
Ecuador	…	…	1714	1714	22.6	−37	1677	20.3	3	1680	19.8	5	1685	18.6	4	1689	18.0
Paraguay	520	16.0	69	589	7.8	76	665	7.8	−2	663	8.1	14	677	7.8	14	691	7.3
Total	3246	100.0	4347	7593	100.0	655	8248	100.0	226	8474	100.0	580	9054	100.0	339	9393	100.0

Source: Adapted from LAFTA, *Síntesis Mensual* (Montevideo: December 1967), p. 601.

than 50 percent of all concessions granted. Peru, however, had granted only 400 concessions as of 1966.

Comparing Tables 4 and 5 we see that Argentina and Brazil account for approximately 60 percent of intrazonal exports and 50–55 percent of the tariff concessions. Peru also acounts for twice the amount of exports and imports as compared to the number of tariff concessions granted during this period. Chile accounts for a larger percentage of intrazonal imports than the cumulative percentage of tariff concessions granted. The share of intrazonal trade held by the remaining countries (Mexico, Colombia, Uruguay, Ecuador, and Paraguay) is less than the percentage of cumulative tariff concessions granted by them. Therefore, the majority of countries have accounted for a larger percentage of tariff concessions than their corresponding percentage of intrazonal trade. The larger countries of Argentina and Brazil, which are in a better trade position because of their economic size and productive ability, account for a disproportionally large share of intrazonal trade relative to the number of concessions they have granted. It appears that intrazonal trade tends to operate in favor of the more developed countries. Peru is the only less developed country that has gained a larger share of exports than the share of tariff concessions she has granted.

Any analysis of the number of specific items on which concessions have been granted that does not take into account the qualitative aspects of a concession is subject to a major bias. That is, a large concession on a major product is much more significant than a minor concession on an unimportant item.[3]

Table 6 gives a breakdown of intrazonal imports of items covered by tariff concessions, and those not covered as compared with extrazonal imports and total Latin American imports. Intrazonal imports of items on which tariff concessions have been granted have increased from 76 percent of total LAFTA intrazonal imports in 1962 to 89 percent in 1965. Correspondingly, intrazonal imports as a percent of total imports of LAFTA have grown from 7 percent in 1962 to 13 percent in 1965. However, imports of negotiated items have decreased relatively from an increase of 9 percentage points between 1962 and 1963 to no change between 1964 and 1965. The tariff negotiations up to 1965,

[3] This point was emphasized by W. V. Turnage, LAFTA *Tariff Concessions and Zonal Trade.*

TABLE 6

EVOLUTION OF INTRAZONAL IMPORTS OF PRODUCTS ON WHICH CONCESSIONS HAVE BEEN NEGOTIATED AND NOT NEGOTIATED

Year	Country	Intrazonal imports Negotiated products $US (1,000)	Percent total	Products not negotiated $US (1,000)	Percent total	Total $US (1,000)	Percent global	Extrazonal imports $US (1,000)	Percent global	Global imports $US (1,000)
1	Argentina	81,349.7	79	21,834.7	21	103,184.4	8	1,253,309.4	92	1,356,493.8
9	Brazil	111,974.8	87	16,619.7	13	128,594.5	9	1,346,060.4	91	1,474,654.9
	Colombia	5,794.0	46	6,728.0	54	12,522.0	2	527,821.0	98	540,343.0
6	Chile	55,110.1	68	25,428.9	32	80,530.0	16	431,301.0	84	511,840.0
	Ecuador	....		3,870.0	100	3,870.0	4	93,277.0	96	97,147.0
2	Mexico	4,140.2	68	1,964.8	32	6,105.0	1	1,136,895.0	99	1,143,000.0
	Paraguay	1,742.1	29	4,307.9	71	6,049.0	15	33,985.0	85	40,034.0
	Peru	33,130.0	73	12,056.0	27	45,186.0	8	491,693.0	92	436,879.0
	Uruguay	26,412.1	78	7,623.9	22	34,036.0	15	196,448.0	85	230,484.0
	Total	319,653.0	76	100,433.9	24	420,086.9	7	5,510,789.8	93	5,930,875.7
1	Argentina	92,502.1	91	9,117.9	9	101,620.0	10	879,048.9	90	980,668.9
9	Brazil	147,304.0	90	16,617.3	10	163,921.3	11	1,322,926.7	89	1,486,848.0
	Colombia	19,547.2	91	1,844.8	9	21,392.0	4	484,640.0	96	506,032.0
6	Chile	93,594.6	78	26,432.4	22	120,027.0	19	517,496.0	81	637,523.0
	Ecuador	4,003.0	77	1,169.0	23	5,172.0	4	123,739.0	96	128,911.0
3	Mexico	9,066.9	84	1,769.1	16	10,836.0	1	1,227,834.0	99	1,238,670.0
	Paraguay	1,847.8	22	6,577.2	78	8,425.0	26	24,179.0	74	32,604.0
	Peru	54,139.4	87	7,860.6	13	62,000.0	11	495,400.0	89	557,400.0
	Uruguay	24,230.4	76	7,520.6	24	31,751.0	18	145,148.0	82	176,899.0
	Total	446,235.4	85	78,908.9	15	525,144.3	9	5,220,411.6	91	5,745,555.9
1	Argentina	157,923.8	93	12,738.7	7	170,662.5	16	906,503.7	84	1,077,166.2
9	Brazil	161,500.3	96	6,460.5	4	167,960.8	13	1,095,489.8	87	1,263,450.6
	Colombia	31,139.0	94	1,960.1	6	33,100.0	6	553,200.0	94	586,300.0
9	Chile	116,093.0	90	12,795.0	10	128,888.0	21	479,920.0	79	608,808.0
	Ecuador	6,453.6	80	1,573.4	20	8,027.0	6	130,034.0	94	138,061.0

TABLE 6 (Continued)

Year	Country	Intrazonal imports						Extrazonal imports		Global imports
		Negotiated products		Products not negotiated		Total				
		$US (1,000)	Percent total	$US (1,000)	Percent total	$US (1,000)	Percent global	$US (1,000)	Percent global	$US (1,000)
6	Mexico	14,967.0	86	2,354.0	14	17,321.0	1	1,475,629.0	99	1,492,950.0
	Paraguay	2,934.8	25	8,624.2	75	11,559.0	29	28,262.0	71	39,821.0
4	Peru	48,958.1	83	9,917.9	17	58,876.0	10	521,124.0	90	580,000.0
	Uruguay	34,987.5	71	14,312.0	29	49,300.0	25	145,100.0	75	194,400.0
	Total	574,958.0	89	70,735.8	11	645,693.8	11	5,335,262.5	89	5,980,956.8
1	Argentina	232,329.6	91	23,370.4	9	255,700.0	21	942,700.0	79	1,198,400.0
	Brazil	182,261.4	96	8,149.6	4	190,411.0	17	906,012.0	83	1,096,423.0
	Colombia	36,001.1	94	2,353.9	6	38,355.0	8	417,190.0	92	455,545.0
9	Chile	113,599.6	93	8,000.4	7	121,600.0	20	482,000.0	80	603,600.0
	Ecuador[1]	6,453.6	80	1,573.4	20	8,027.0	6	130,034.0	94	138,061.0
6	Mexico	21,097.3	71	8,576.7	29	29,674.0	2	1,530,547.0	98	1,560,221.0
	Paraguay	2,503.2	22	8,887.8	78	11,391.0	22	40,274.0	78	51,665.0
5	Peru	62,791.3	78	18,108.7	22	80,900.0	11	649,000.0	89	729,900.0
	Uruguay	26,349.8	82	5,733.2	18	32,083.0	27	118,666.0	73	150,749.0
	Total	683,386.9	89	84,754.1	11	768,141.0	13	5,216,423.0	87	5,984,564.0
	Argentina	No Data Exist				226,674	20	897,632.0	80	1,124,306.0
	Brazil					167,043	11	1,329,172.0	89	1,496,215.0
1	Colombia					56,029	8	618,236.0	92	674,265.0
	Chile					123,912	18	561,376.0	82	685,288.0
9	Ecuador					8,349	5	163,566.0	95	171,915.0
	Mexico					33,693	2	1,571,467.0	98	1,605,160.0
6	Paraguay					14,317	24	43,672.0	76	57,989.0
	Peru					91,481	11	125,431.0	89	816,912.0
6	Uruguay					46,030	28	118,212.0	72	164,242.0
	Total					767,528	11	6,928,764.0	89	6,796,292.0

[1] The 1964 figure is repeated since no 1965 data are available.

Source: LAFTA (Cómite Ejecutivo Permanente), *Sumario Comercio Intrazonal Generado en el Programa de Liberación del Tratado de Montevideo*, CEP/Repartido 856 (Montevideo: July 5, 1967), pp. 21–22.

therefore, seem to have had a positive effect on expanding intrazonal trade. Specifically, regional trade in products on which tariff concessions have been extended more than doubled (from $319 million in 1962 to $683 million in 1965) while trade in nonnegotiated products declined (from $100 million in 1962 to $84 million in 1965). Nevertheless, with the decrease in the number of tariff concessions granted, a corresponding slowdown seems apparent—as shown by the 1966 data—in the total value of intrazonal imports as well as in its percent of total LAFTA imports.

Most of the intrazonal trade has been in basic agricultural and primary products and only a relatively small amount represented manufactured items. Although animal, vegetable, wood, textile, and metal products accounted for more than 70 percent of total LAFTA trade, only about 25 percent of all concessions apply to these products. The greatest number of concessions have been in the manufacturing area, where chemicals and machinery alone account for about 50 percent of all concessions. These products, comprising less than 10 percent of intrazonal trade, have been experiencing a very high rate of growth. Although intrazonal trade in basic agricultural and metal materials has also grown, the rate of growth has been less than that of manufactures.[4]

These concessions, in varying proportions, relate to nearly all the major tariff items—particularly chemicals, machinery, electrical appliances and supplies, basic metals and manufactures, agricultural commodities, and processed agricultural products. Still on complete sections of NABALALC, however, practically no tariff concessions have been granted, or if so, on only a very small scale and by one country. Most of the concessions adopted so far relate to products that are not very highly processed. The effect of this is to boost existing trade flows instead of creating the conditions required for the dynamic expansion of new items.

The foregoing suggests that the intrazonal concessions and preferential treatment have not only improved zonal trade in such products as food and raw materials, which are customarily purchased by the members of the zone, but also have induced the LAFTA countries to replace their imports of these and other products from outside the

---

[4] For a more extensive treatment see W. V. Turnage, LAFTA *Tariff Concessions and Zonal Trade*, pp. 1–5.

zone. That is, imports from third countries have been increasingly replaced by purchases of those items from other members. As a result of these changes, the increase of over $145 million in all negotiated items imported from the area between 1961 and 1964 contrasts with the reduction of nearly $50 million in imports of the same products from the rest of the world.[5]

Certain provisions of the Treaty are expressly aimed at facilitating the granting of exclusive customs benefits to countries at a relatively less advanced stage of economic development, mainly Ecuador and Paraguay. In this respect the other member countries of LAFTA have granted nearly 7,000 tariff concessions in favor of these countries. The purpose of this preferential treatment is to promote exports from the less developed countries to the rest of the area to encourage the establishment of new industries for processing their raw materials.

The Seventh Conference of Contracting Parties (October 23 to December 18, 1967) witnessed the addition of a relatively large number of new tariff concessions to the National Lists. Member countries agreed to more than 700 general concessions and about 600 special concessions applicable to the less developed countries. This is the largest addition of negotiated concessions to the National Lists in any single year since 1963.[6]

Although a major portion of the increase in intrazonal trade unquestionably should be ascribed to tariff cutting, improvements in payments arrangements also contributed to this trend.[7] The foregoing comparisons illustrate the effectiveness of regional agreements in promoting reciprocal trade, since most of the increase took place in trade between the member countries. In short, trade liberalization, reinforced with other action, resulted in the significantly greater intraregional trade that had been sought in the interests of development.[8]

---

[5] Information in the above two paragraphs is from UN, *Economic Survey of Latin America, 1965*, pp. 46–52.

[6] See W. V. Turnage, *Seventh LAFTA Conference (1967)*.

[7] LAFTA is evolving a zonal-payment system, based on a network of bilateral agreements between central banks. Early experience with the system, initiated only in 1966, indicates multilateralized compensation arrangements embracing something over 30 percent of potentially coverable transactions.

[8] There is now a proposal in LAFTA to progressively reduce tariffs on items on the Common List, beginning in 1969.

In addition to the removal of tariff restrictions by means of National Lists, the Treaty also requires that every three years 25 percent of the items traded be added to a Common List. In 1973 every item on the Common List will be freely traded within the zone. The first additions to the Common List came in 1964; the second addition, due in 1967, has encountered some difficulty. With intensified efforts to develop a common market, the Common List now takes on a new potential of great importance, since the items included there may be those to which the automatic tariff-reduction process first applies. Although the proposed items have been submitted for the second round of additions to the Common List, no conclusions have as yet been reached and negotiations, continued into 1968, may extend into 1969.[9]

Since the Seventh LAFTA Conference did not reach agreement on the Common List a later meeting was scheduled for July 1968. During the Seventh Conference primary effort was devoted to the inclusion on the Common List of wheat and petroleum, which together account for more than 25 percent of intraregional trade. For various reasons, not all members could agree to include wheat or petroleum, or both, on the Common List. In some cases state trading in these items, which makes tariff controls more or less irrelevant, presented an obstacle to agreement. In other cases, the protection of local production, which tends to be high-cost, presented a problem. It may be that petroleum will not be taken into account, although wheat, through a compromise plan, may be in the computation of the second Common List. The compromise would be that some countries would list objections in the final document, but would not block the entire agreement.[10]

[9] Most countries have proposed some major export items for inclusion on the second Common List. For example: Argentina has proposed wheat; Chile, newsprint and copper; Colombia, cattle, meat, tires, and tubes; Peru, lead and zinc; and Uruguay, sand, wool tops, and meat. Venezuela has included a number of chemical items, which are not as yet traded in the zone in large quantity. Some manufactured products and machinery have been included by Mexico, and Brazil has proposed iron and steel. Argentina's proposed list amounted to almost half the value of regional trade involved in the group of proposals, and the number of items was substantially larger than proposed by any other country. The larger the number of items, even those not yet traded in appreciable quantity, the larger the scope of an automatic system of tariff reduction. For a more expanded treatment see W. V. Turnage, LAFTA Notes, pp. 1–7.

[10] See W. V. Turnage, *Seventh* LAFTA *Conference (1967)*.

The future success of freeing up intrazonal trade depends directly on establishing and implementing some program of automatic tariff reductions. At the 1967 meeting of the Council of Ministers such a program was seriously discussed, with the resulting adoption of Resolution 191.[11] In general this resolution called for: (1) continued consideration of programed tariff reductions, (2) consolidation and simplification of tariffs and other restrictions, (3) tariff reductions for items on the Common List, (4) margins of preference within LAFTA, and (5) examination of problems concerning a common external tariff and common LAFTA attitudes before third countries and international organizations.[12]

More specifically it was generally agreed that the automatic tariff-reduction process should proceed at differential rates for the products of each of the three groups of countries. Although agreement was not reached on the specific rates with which each group reduction should proceed, two programs of automatic tariff reductions have since been suggested and are presented in Figures 9 and 10. In each case the importance of national diversity is taken into consideration with different rates of reduction for each category of country. Under both programs special concessions are planned for the relatively less developed and the insufficient-market countries. The program presented in Figure 9 would seem to involve more integrating spirit for the countries concerned than the more direct program in Figure 10, but at the same time the first plan may prove more difficult to implement.

Besides the problems inherent in the reduction of the barriers to intrazonal trade, the achievement of free trade within the region is handicapped by the problem of currency instability among the member countries. This problem, expressed through inflation and balance-of-payments difficulties, hampers investment and economic development in the region by interfering with the market mechanism. It also has a direct influence on foreign exports by supporting a deterioration in the terms of trade between raw materials and industrial goods. Many feel that these exchange rates have promoted virtually no exports in manufacturing, since "one exchange rate will move all

[11] LAFTA, *Sintesis Mensual*, October 1967, p. 496.

[12] For an elaboration of these points, see W. V. Turnage, LAFTA *Developments, 1967*.

Figure 9

TARIFF REDUCTION PROGRAM FOR THE OPENING OF MARKETS AT DIFFERENT RATES (IN PERCENTAGES)

GRADUAL AND SIMULTANEOUS

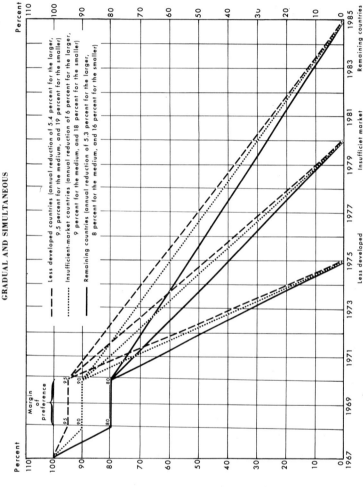

Source: Pan American Union, Statistical Office.

74

Tariffs Remaining in Each Year (Percentages)

Year	Less developed countries to:			Insufficient-market countries to:			Remaining countries to:		
	Less developed countries	Insufficient-market countries	Remaining countries	Less developed countries	Insufficient-market countries	Remaining countries	Less developed countries	Insufficient-market countries	Remaining countries
1971	76	85.5	88.7	72	81	84	64	72	74.7
1972	57	76.0	82.4	54	72	78	48	64	69.4
1973	38	66.5	76.1	36	63	72	32	56	64.1
1974	19	57.0	69.8	18	54	66	16	48	58.8
1975	0	47.5	63.5	0	45	60	0	40	53.5
1976		38.0	57.2		36	54		32	46.2
1977		28.5	50.9		27	48		24	42.9
1978		19.5	44.6		18	42		16	37.6
1979		9.5	38.3		9	36		8	32.3
1980		0	32.0		0	30		0	27.0
1981			25.7			24			21.7
1982			19.4			18			16.4
1983			13.1			12			11.1
1984			6.8			6			5.8
1985			0			0			0

Figure 10

TARIFF-REDUCTION PROGRAM WITH DIFFERING RATES OF REDUCTION (IN PERCENTAGES)

DURING THE ENTIRE PERIOD

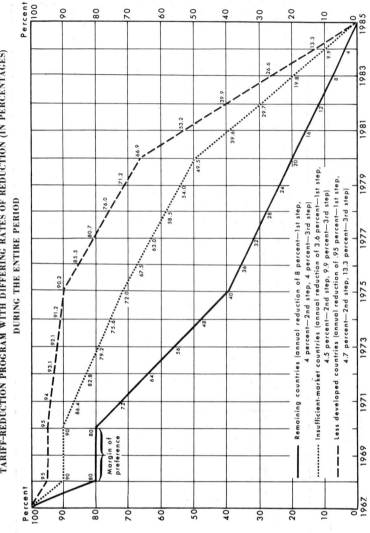

Source: Pan American Union, Statistical Office.

76

Tariffs Remaining in Each Year (Percentages)

Year	Less developed countries	Insufficient-market countries	Remaining countries	Year	Less developed countries	Insufficient-market countries	Remaining countries
1970	95.0	90.0	80	1978	76.0	58.5	28
1971	94.0	86.4	72	1979	71.2	54.0	24
1972	93.1	82.8	64	1980	66.5	49.5	20
1973	92.1	79.2	56	1981	53.2	39.6	16
1974	91.2	75.6	48	1982	39.9	29.7	12
1975	90.2	72.0	40	1983	26.6	19.8	8
1976	85.5	67.5	36	1984	13.3	9.9	4
1977	80.7	63.0	32	1985	0	0	0

the basic products demanded but a more depreciated rate seems to be needed to move non-traditional export items."[13] To overcome this problem in their foreign-trade relations some countries have adopted a multiple-exchange-rate system. Intrazonal trade, however, is sensitive to relative prices within each country and currency instability is a problem for both supplying and demanding countries. Under these conditions any long-range planning by entrepreneurs, for either supply or demand, is especially difficult.

An examination of currency instability, as represented by the exchange rate and the cost-of-living index, shows that it is in most cases a direct cause of fluctuations or shifts in intrazonal trade. The relative competitive position of each country changes directly with domestic price fluctuations in each country, thus causing shifts in the direction of intrazonal trade. In the short run devaluation tends to attract intrazonal trade in favor of the devaluing country. In the long run the country that is able to maintain its currency and price stability, such as Mexico, experiences a more rapid and sustained increase in the volume of intrazonal exports than do countries with less stable money situations.[14]

[13] W. V. Turnage, LAFTA Developments, 1967, p. 7. For a more extensive treatment see W. V. Turnage, "Unstable Currencies Hamper LAFTA Trade Growth, Cloud Picture for U.S. Traders and Investors," International Commerce, September 25, 1967, pp. 8–10.

[14] This relation between exchange rates and intrazonal trade is modified to some extent because most of the intrazonal trade is in items which can be produced only by certain countries or which are priced by world markets.

EXTRAZONAL TRADE OF LAFTA

Because of the need for foreign exchange to obtain imports of needed capital equipment, extraregional exports, as mentioned earlier, are most important to the success of LAFTA and the economic development of the area. While it is desirable to develop industry supporting the expansion of intraregional imports in order to save foreign exchange, recent economic-development trends and writings indicate also a need for export-creating or foreign-exchange-earning industries. Intraregional trade should not be expanded at the expense of extrazonal exports but rather with the encouragement of the latter. For the developing countries of LAFTA and their relation with nonmember countries it is most important that trade-creating effects result so that member countries can earn foreign exchange in order to finance more industrialization, and pay the rapidly rising costs of debt services. The importance of extraregional imports is emphasized by the fact that they account for almost 90 percent of the imports of LAFTA countries, and tariffs on them are a major source of revenue for governments.

Table 7 shows the value and the member-country distribution of extrazonal trade of LAFTA. In a comparison of the earlier results of intraregional trade with those of extraregional trade it is important to realize that, although the rate of increase has been larger in the case of intraregional exports, extrazonal exports account for about 90 percent of the value of LAFTA's total trade. Thus, with each one-dollar increase of intrazonal exports, extraregional exports increased more than six dollars. Since the signing of the Treaty intraregional exports have increased about $55 million in 1962, $70 million in 1963, $125 million in 1964, $80 million in 1965, and $40 million in 1966. During the same years the increase in extraregional exports in millions of dollars was 210, 218, 282, 505, and 414 respectively. Even though exports to both regional markets and extraregional markets increased about the same percentage in 1966, the value difference of the increases is $360 million in favor of extraregional exports. From 1961 to 1966 LAFTA exports to regional markets increased by $375 million, but the increase to extraregional markets was about $1.6 billion.

79

Table 7 shows that trade with countries outside the region increased significantly between 1934/38 and 1946/51. Thereafter, this pattern changed radically, with the export trend continuing to increase, but at a much slower rate, while the import trend leveled off. This downturn in the extra-regional-trade trend is more clearly seen in Figures 11 and 12. The cumulative rate of growth, for both exports and imports, was greater between 1946/51 and 1966 than between 1961 and 1966. In both periods the cumulative rate of export growth was larger than that for imports, whose rate of change has been decreasing for most countries since 1961. Extrazonal exports increased more than 100 percent between 1961 and 1966.

National distribution of extraregional trade shows that Argentina, Brazil, and Mexico together account for over 60 percent of all exports and imports, with the relative shares of Argentina and Mexico continuing to grow in exports since 1961. Colombia, Chile, and Peru account for over 30 percent of extraregional trade, while Uruguay, Ecuador, and Paraguay are responsible for about 10 percent. Extraregional exports for Argentina, Brazil, and Uruguay represent approximately 85 percent of total exports from these countries, and for Paraguay 60 percent, while for other member countries the share is approximately 93 to 94 percent of their total exports.[1]

In contrast to the substantial increase noted above in exports to non-LAFTA markets, extraregional imports in the period since 1961 increased less than 10 percent, and decreased in several countries. In fact, Argentina, Brazil, and Uruguay experienced significant decreases in imports from non-LAFTA countries, while Colombia, Chile, and Paraguay showed sharply fluctuating import figures. This decrease in extraregional imports is directly or indirectly related to the shortage of foreign exchange, expansion of import-substitution industries, and the development of an alternative course of imports in intrazonal trade.[2]

[1] According to the UN, *Economic Survey of Latin America, 1965*, pp. 67–70, LAFTA countries can be arranged in three groups with respect to extrazonal exports: (1) Brazil and Paraguay—having a growth rate of current export earnings between 11.5 and 15 percent; (2) Argentina, Mexico, Chile, and Uruguay—with a growth rate between 4.5 and 8.5 percent; and (3) Colombia, Peru, and Ecuador—whose value of exports remained virtually unchanged.

[2] For a further discussion of the foreign-trade problems and policies of Latin America and LAFTA see Pan American Union, *Latin America's Foreign Trade Policy* and Roy Blough, Jack N. Behrman, and Romulo A. Ferrero, *Regional Integration and the Trade of Latin America.*

TABLE 7

LAFTA: EXTRAZONAL TRADE BY COUNTRY, 1934–1966
(Value in millions of $U.S.)
EXPORTS (f.o.b.)

	1934–1938 Value	Percent	1946–1951 Value	Percent	1952 Value	Percent	1953–1955 Value	Percent	1956–1958 Value	Percent	1959–1961 Value	Percent	1961 Value	Percent	1946/51–1966 Percentage change	1961–66 Percentage change
Argentina	540	37.8	1,313	32.3	743	17.7	822	18.8	848	19.4	884	19.7	864	18.5	3	56
Brazil	304	21.3	1,242	30.5	1,408	33.6	1,376	31.5	1,245	28.5	1,233	27.6	1,308	28.0	26	19
Mexico	207	14.4	439	10.8	546	13.0	677	15.5	776	17.8	774	17.3	817	17.5	167	43
Chile	129	9.0	303	7.4	462	11.0	370	8.4	428	9.8	463	10.4	473	10.1	172	74
Colombia	78	5.5	320	7.8	473	11.3	609	13.9	520	11.9	454	10.2	429	9.2	49	11
Peru	80	5.6	178	4.3	239	5.7	194	4.4	261	5.9	375	8.3	463	9.9	299	54
Uruguay	69	4.8	196	4.8	209	4.9	205	4.6	142	3.2	130	2.9	169	3.6	−19	−6
Ecuador	13	.9	47	1.1	77	1.8	100	2.3	118	2.7	131	2.9	120	2.5	177	8
Paraguay	8	.5	28	.6	29	.6	20	.4	22	.5	22	.5	21	.4	3	38
Total[1]	1,428	100.0	4,066	100.0	4,186	100.0	4,373	100.0	4,360	100.0	4,466	100.0	4,664	100.0	57	37

	1962 Value	Percent	1963 Value	Percent	1964 Value	Percent	1965 Value	Percent	1966 Value	Percent
Argentina	1,075	22.0	1,180	22.9	1,192	21.4	1,261	22.0	1,350	21.0
Brazil	1,138	23.4	1,331	25.9	1,300	23.4	1,398	24.4	1,559	24.3
Mexico	913	18.7	958	18.7	1,019	18.3	963	16.8	1,171	18.3
Chile	493	10.1	493	9.4	572	10.3	634	11.0	823	12.8
Colombia	456	9.3	440	8.5	537	9.6	522	9.1	477	7.4
Peru	489	10.0	491	9.5	603	10.8	613	10.7	711	11.1
Uruguay	145	2.9	150	2.9	164	2.9	176	3.0	159	2.5
Ecuador	137	2.8	58	1.1	137	2.4	120	2.0	130	2.0
Paraguay	23	.4	30	.6	35	.6	40	.7	29	.5
Total[1]	4,869	100.0	5,131	100.0	5,559	100.0	5,727	100.0	6,409	100.0

[1] Total differs from sum because of rounding.

Source: UN, Yearbook of International Trade Statistics (various issues), Table A.

TABLE 7 (Continued)

LAFTA: EXTRAZONAL TRADE BY COUNTRY, 1934-1966
(Value in millions of $U.S.)

IMPORTS (c.i.f.)

	1934-1938		1946-1951		1952		1953-1955		1956-1958		1959-1961		1961	
	Value	Percent	Value	Percent	Value	Percent	Value	Percent	Value	Percent	Value	Percent	Value	Percent
Argentina	377	35.9	1,163	28.5	1,136	21.9	796	18.6	1,060	21.7	1,121	21.9	1,334	23.6
Brazil	260	24.8	1,210	29.6	2,009	38.8	1,232	28.8	1,246	25.5	1,342	26.2	1,415	25.0
Mexico	126	12.0	611	14.9	607	11.7	828	19.3	1,116	22.8	1,106	21.6	1,135	20.0
Chile	75	7.1	269	6.6	371	7.2	271	6.3	348	7.1	424	8.3	496	8.8
Colombia	78	7.4	368	9.0	415	8.0	613	14.3	502	10.3	489	9.6	547	9.6
Peru	51	4.8	176	4.3	287	5.4	260	6.1	341	6.9	351	6.8	436	7.7
Uruguay	61	5.8	209	5.1	246	4.7	179	4.2	171	3.5	173	3.4	174	3.1
Ecuador	12	1.1	49	1.2	66	1.2	81	1.9	87	1.8	91	1.8	90	1.6
Paraguay	10	.9	27	.6	38	.7	18	.4	17	.3	22	.4	25	.4
Total[1]	1,050	100.0	4,082	100.0	5,175	100.0	4,278	100.0	4,888	100.0	5,119	100.0	5,652	100.0

	1962		1963		1964		1965		1966		1946/51–1966 Percentage change	1961–66 Percentage change
	Value	Percent	Value	Percent	Value	Percent	Value	Percent	Value	Percent		
Argentina	1,254	22.8	880	16.9	907	16.9	945	18.1	897	14.8	-23	-33
Brazil	1,347	24.5	1,323	25.5	1,095	20.5	906	17.4	1,329	21.9	10	-6
Mexico	1,137	20.7	1,229	23.7	1,476	27.7	1,531	29.4	1,571	25.9	157	38
Chile	432	7.8	517	9.9	480	8.9	482	9.2	614	10.1	128	24
Colombia	528	9.6	485	9.4	553	10.4	416	7.9	618	10.2	68	13
Peru	489	8.9	471	9.1	512	9.6	638	12.2	726	11.9	313	66
Uruguay	197	3.6	145	2.8	149	2.8	119	2.3	118	1.9	-44	-32
Ecuador	81	1.5	108	2.1	141	2.6	143	2.7	143	2.4	192	59
Paraguay	28	.5	26	.5	23	.4	31	.6	44	.7	63	76
Total[1]	5,493	100.0	5,184	100.0	5,336	100.0	5,211	100.0	6,060	100.0	48	7

[1] Total differs from sum because of rounding.

Source: UN, *Yearbook of International Trade Statistics* (various issues), Table A.

Figure 11

**RATE OF CHANGE AND DISTRIBUTION OF EXTRAZONAL EXPORTS
BY COUNTRY, 1948-1965 (F.O.B. VALUE)**

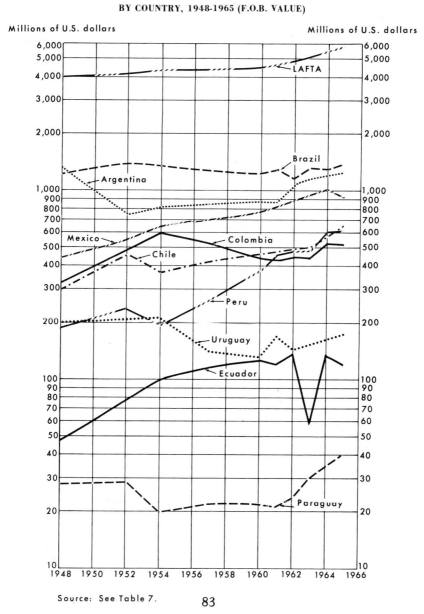

Millions of U.S. dollars

Millions of U.S. dollars

Source: See Table 7.

83

Figure 12

RATE OF CHANGE AND DISTRIBUTION OF EXTRAZONAL IMPORTS
BY COUNTRY, 1948-1965 (C.I.F. VALUE)

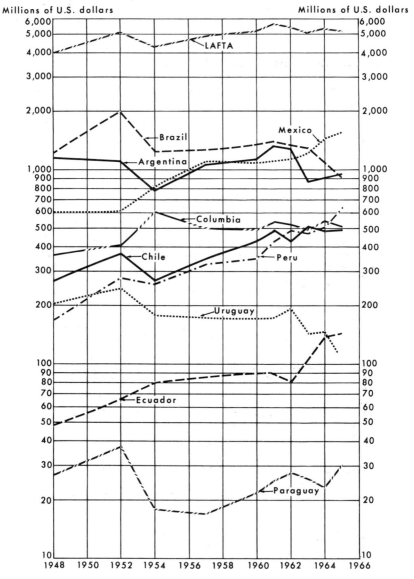

Source: See Table 7.

PER CAPITA INCOME AND PRODUCTIVITY

Another important test of the developmental impact of economic integration is the degree of change in per capita income and in productivity of the major sectors of the economy. Table 8 shows the total and per capita production at constant prices between 1950 and 1965, expressed as percentages of 1958 values. With 1958 as the base year, it is apparent that between 1950 and 1965 the more developed countries have experienced the greatest increase in per capita income: for Mexico the increase in the percentage relative of 1965 over that of 1950 is 39 percentage points of the base, or a 50-percent gain during the period; for Brazil, the difference in relatives is 31 points, or a 37.3-percent gain; and for Argentina, 19 points, or a 21.6-percent gain. Other significant increases in per capita income during the period have been experienced by Peru (33 points, or a 35.9-percent gain), Paraguay (32 points, or a 43.8-percent gain), Colombia (25 points, or a 29.5-percent gain), Chile (17 points, or an 18.3-percent gain), Ecuador (16 points, or a 17.0-percent gain), and Uruguay (6 points, or a 6.8-percent gain). However, if we concentrate attention on the period between 1960 and 1965 we find that the more developed countries have experienced the greatest gains. For instance, the greatest increase in per capita income was experienced by Peru with a 16.8-percent gain; Chile had a 15.8-percent gain, Mexico a 12.5-percent gain, and Argentina a 9.2-percent gain. Brazil and Paraguay both experienced a small 7-percent gain, while the smallest increases in per capita income were experienced by Colombia, with a 5.7-percent gain, Uruguay, with a 4.1-percent gain, and Ecuador, with a 3.7-percent gain.

Table 9 shows the evolution and structure of the sectoral product for Latin America between 1950 and 1965. It was during the period 1955–1960 that the changes in Latin American production were most rapid. During this period the importance of agriculture sharply decreased while that of manufacturing increased. The cumulative rates of growth of any sector between 1960 and 1965 show no spectacular increase but rather continual decline in most cases.

Annual growth rates between 1961 and 1966 for individual sectors are presented in Figure 13 supported by Table 10 (data range = 1960–

TABLE 8

TOTAL AND PER CAPITA PRODUCT AT CONSTANT PRICES[1], 1950–1965
(Percentage relatives, 1958 = 100)

	1950 Total	Per cap.	1953 Total	Per cap.	1955 Total	Per cap.	1956 Total	Per cap.	1957 Total	Per cap.	1959 Total	Per cap.	1960 Total	Per cap.	1961 Total	Per cap.	1962 Total	Per cap.	1963 Total	Per cap.	1964 Total	Per cap.	1965 Total	Per cap.
Argentina	75	88	78	86	87	82	88	92	93	95	94	93	102	98	109	104	107	100	103	95	111	101	120	107
Brazil[2]	65	83	75	87	86	94	88	93	94	97	107	104	114	106	123	110	129	113	131	112	136	112	142	114
Mexico[2]	61	78	69	80	83	91	88	94	95	98	103	99	111	104	115	104	121	106	128	108	141	116	149	117
Chile[3]	77	93	89	101	85	92	90	94	99	102	103	100	100	95	108	100	116	105	119	106	125	109	129	110
Colombia	71	85	83	92	92	98	95	100	98	101	107	104	111	104	116	106	122	108	126	108	134	111	138	110
Peru[4]	77	92	87	98	93	101	94	99	97	99	104	101	113	107	122	112	133	119	139	120	149	125	...	...
Uruguay	70	88	81	94	101	104	103	105	104	105	97	96	101	98	104	100	101	96	100	94	102	94	...	...
Ecuador	78	94	81	91	90	98	93	99	97	100	105	102	112	106	115	105	121	107	124	107	133	111	138	110
Paraguay[2]	53	73	67	81	90	97	89	93	95	97	100	97	101	98	107	100	113	103	115	102	119	102	126	105

[1] Domestic product at constant factor cost.
[2] Gross domestic product at market prices.
[3] Net domestic product at factor cost.
[4] G.N.P. at factor cost.
Source: UN, *Statistical Yearbook 1966* (New York: 1967), Table 178.

TABLE 9

LATIN AMERICA: EVOLUTION AND STRUCTURE OF SECTORAL PRODUCT, 1950–1965[1]

Sector	Percentage of total gross product				Cumulative annual growth rates (percentages)			
	1950	1955	1960	1965	1950–55	1955–60	1960–65	1950–65
1. Agriculture, forestry, and fishing	24.6	23.8	21.7	21.8	4.1	2.7	4.8	3.8
2. Mining and quarrying	4.0	4.5	4.9	4.9	7.0	6.9	4.3	6.0
3. Manufacturing	18.7	19.7	21.7	22.7	6.0	6.6	5.6	6.1
4. Construction	3.4	3.4	3.3	3.2	5.0	4.2	4.3	4.5
5. Electricity, gas, and water	0.7	0.8	1.0	1.4	7.8	9.3	10.5	9.2
6. Transport and communications	6.3	6.6	6.4	6.2	5.7	4.1	4.2	4.6
Subtotal for basic goods and services	57.7	58.8	59.1	60.2	..	..	..	..
Weighted average for basic goods and services	..	..	..	..	5.2	4.7	5.1	5.0
7. Trade and finance	17.3	17.7	18.0	17.8	5.3	4.8	4.6	4.9
8. Public administration and defense	8.6	7.8	7.1	6.5	2.9	2.6	2.9	2.8
9. Other services	16.4	15.7	15.9	15.5	3.9	4.8	4.2	4.3
Total for all sectors	100.0	100.0	100.0	100.0	..	..	..	..
Weighted average for all sectors	..	..	..	..	4.8	4.6	4.7	4.7

[1] Estimates based on gross product at factor cost.

Source: UN, *Economic Survey of Latin America, 1965* (New York: 1967).

TABLE 10

LATIN AMERICA: RECENT EVOLUTION OF SECTORAL PRODUCT, 1960–1965[1]

(Percentages)

Sector	1960–61	1961–62	Annual growth rates 1962–63	1963–64	1964–65
1. Agriculture, forestry, and fishing	4.6	4.2	1.7	4.0	9.6
2. Mining and quarrying	3.0	6.0	2.7	6.8	3.3
3. Manufacturing	7.8	3.2	1.3	9.8	6.3
4. Construction	2.3	1.4	4.1	8.9	4.7
5. Electricity, gas, and water	12.1	11.0	10.5	9.5	9.5
6. Transport and communications	5.5	2.9	2.3	6.0	4.2
Weighted average for basic goods and services	5.7	3.8	2.0	7.0	7.0
7. Trade and finance	6.6	2.8	1.1	6.1	6.3
8. Public administration and defense	2.7	2.0	3.5	3.1	3.4
9. Other services	3.5	3.7	4.6	4.8	4.4
Weighted average for all sectors	5.3	3.5	2.3	6.2	6.2

[1] Estimates based on gross product at factor cost.
Source: UN, *Economic Survey of Latin America, 1965* (New York: 1967).

Figure 13

LATIN AMERICA: SELECTED SECTORAL
GROWTH RATES, 1961-1966

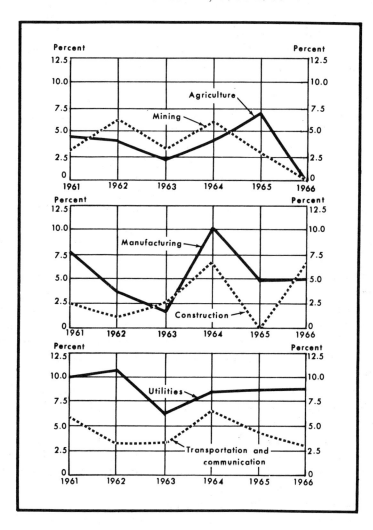

Source: UCLA (Latin American Center), *Statistical Abstract of Latin America, 1966* (October 1967), p. 21.

89

1965). Agriculture, the most important sector in Latin America, shows a sharp decrease since 1964, mostly because of reduced output in Brazil and Argentina, and continual competition in agricultural exports from the African countries in the production of coffee, cotton, and cacao. As the trend to greater national participation in processing natural resources continued in Latin America, growth in the mining sector continued to be very rapid.

Investment in dynamic rather than slow-growth industries supported the 1963 expansion of growth in the manufacturing sector. Specifically, the increase in steel-ingot production, rolled products, manufacture of motor vehicles, and to a lesser extent in the production of fertilizers, plastics, man-made fibers, synthetic rubber, pulp, and paper caused the reversal of trend in the manufacturing sector. However, the average rate of growth of manufacturing between 1960 and 1965 is down about one percent from the 1955–1960 average.

The rates of growth in the construction and the transportation and communication sectors are up slightly from the 1955–1960 average but still below the 1950–1965 average. The continued increase in utilities after 1950–1965 seems to be slowing down slightly since 1963.

In Table 11, which compares the ratio between sectoral growth and the growth of gross product for Latin America, only agriculture and utilities increased significantly in 1960–1965 over the earlier period 1950–1960. During 1950–1955 the following sectors had a ratio value greater than one: mining, manufacturing, construction, utilities, transportation, and trade. Between 1950 and 1960 mining, manufacturing, utilities, and trade had a ratio greater than one, and from 1960 to 1965 only agriculture, manufacturing, and utilities had a ratio larger than one.

Table 12 presents a breakdown by country of gross domestic product growth rates by sector of economic activity between 1955 and 1965. In the agricultural sector Brazil's gross agricultural product accounted for about 40 percent of the whole region's agricultural product in 1965. This same year, Brazil's agricultural activity expanded in the aggregate by 20 percent while, on average, agricultural production in the other countries increased by 3.7 percent.

During that same year in the mining sector considerable increases in the growth rate (12 to 20 percent) were achieved in Brazil, Colom-

90

TABLE 11

LATIN AMERICA: RATIO BETWEEN SECTORAL GROWTH AND GROWTH
OF TOTAL GROSS PRODUCT, BY PERIOD, 1950–1965[1]

Sector	1950–55	1955–60	1960–65	1950–65
1. Agriculture, forestry, and fishing	0.85	0.59	1.02	0.81
2. Mining and quarrying	1.46	1.50	0.91	1.28
3. Manufacturing	1.25	1.43	1.19	1.30
4. Construction	1.04	0.91	0.91	0.96
5. Electricity, gas, and water	1.62	2.02	2.23	1.96
6. Transport and communications	1.19	0.89	0.89	0.98
Weighted average for basic goods and services	1.08	1.02	1.09	1.06
7. Trade and finance	1.10	1.04	0.98	1.04
8. Public administration and defense	0.60	0.57	0.62	0.60
9. Other services	0.81	1.04	0.89	0.91
Weighted average for all sectors	1.00	1.00	1.00	1.00

[1] Estimates based on gross product at factor cost.
Source: UN, *Economic Survey of Latin America, 1965* (New York: 1967).

TABLE 12

LAFTA: PERCENTAGE GROWTH RATES OF GROSS DOMESTIC
PRODUCT BY SECTOR OF ECONOMIC ACTIVITY, 1955–1965[1]

Country	Agriculture, forestry, hunting, and fishing	Mining and quarrying	Manu- facturing	Con- struction	Electricity, gas, and water	Other sectors	Total
Argentina							
1955–60	−0.4	14.3	3.8	4.3	6.1	2.8	2.7
1960–65	2.1	7.9	4.1	2.0	12.0	1.9	2.8
1963–64	9.6	4.8	14.3	8.9	9.9	4.4	8.6
1964–65	4.0	2.9	11.6	10.3	12.4	6.3	7.8
Brazil							
1955–60	3.7	14.9	10.3	7.2	10.8	4.6	5.9
1960–65	6.9	11.1	4.9	2.8	9.7	3.6	4.9
1963–64	1.3	18.4	5.1	2.1	7.0	3.1	3.1
1964–65	20.0	12.0	1.0	0.7	4.9	3.2	7.3
Mexico							
1955–60	3.0	6.1	8.1	8.1	6.5	6.6	6.1
1960–65	3.9	4.2	8.0	5.9	10.0	6.0	5.9
1963–64	6.2	6.2	14.2	16.4	14.9	9.2	10.1
1964–65	3.1	2.7	7.0	−3.1	9.5	5.9	5.2
Chile							
1955–60	2.3	3.5	3.2	1.4	3.5	3.7	4.3
1960–65	3.1	5.0	6.7	4.6	7.4	5.6	3.5
1963–64	6.4	6.3	5.0	−8.0	10.4	2.3	3.1
1964–65	−1.0	0.0	5.4	10.0	5.6	4.5	4.2
Colombia							
1955–60	3.5	6.8	6.1	−0.2	11.7	3.5	3.9
1960–65	3.0	4.4	5.9	1.9	9.2	5.2	4.5
1963–64	5.1	4.6	6.8	−2.2	6.5	5.3	5.3
1964–65	1.5	13.0	5.4	−4.7	9.2	4.4	3.9
Peru							
1955–60	3.8	11.9	6.1	−2.0	..[2]	4.1	4.7
1960–65	5.9	2.6	7.4	13.3	..[2]	6.1	6.3
1963–64	4.6	3.1	5.6	10.4	..[2]	5.5	5.4
1964–65	5.7	2.3	7.1	12.9	..[2]	5.6	6.0
Uruguay							
1955–60	−3.6	..[3]	0.9	0.1	4.7	0.2	−0.1
1960–65	1.9	..[3]	0.2	−9.1	4.7	0.5	0.4
1963–64	−9.3	..[3]	5.4	−7.4	8.2	2.4	1.1
1964–65	1.2	..[3]	−0.7	−2.3	−2.7	0.9	1.1
Venezuela							
1955–60	6.1	6.6	9.1	1.1	18.1	6.0	6.7

Table 12—Continued

Country	Agriculture, forestry, hunting, and fishing	Mining and quarrying	Manu-facturing	Con-struction	Electricity, gas, and water	Other sectors	Total
1960–65	6.6	3.7	9.4	7.9	12.0	4.6	5.4
1963–64	6.1	7.1	11.3	15.6	9.8	7.0	7.0
1964–65	7.5	2.5	10.7	17.0	12.1	6.3	7.0
Bolivia							
1955–60	2.8	−6.8	−5.0	7.5	. .¹	0.5	−0.3
1960–65	2.0	5.9	6.0	9.3	7.6	5.3	4.8
1963–64	2.0	11.3	10.7	2.6	4.2	5.3	5.5
1964–65	−1.4	4.9	4.0	25.0	4.0	5.5	4.2
Ecuador							
1955–60	4.5	4.7	5.6	10.6	5.8	3.7	4.6
1960–65	2.9	3.0	6.3	3.6	8.6	2.9	3.8
1963–64	2.2	11.5	13.3	14.3	7.1	4.8	5.7
1964–65	3.7	2.9	6.3	3.7	8.3	3.0	3.8
Paraguay							
1955–60	1.8	0.0	1.2	10.5	11.0	2.3	2.2
1960–65	4.0	8.5	5.9	2.2	4.7	4.0	4.3
1963–64	7.2	0.0	4.3	2.4	3.2	5.1	6.6
1964–65	3.7	20.0	9.0	2.3	6.3	5.5	4.5
Latin America							
1955–60	2.7	6.8	6.6	4.2	9.4	4.4	4.6
1960–65	4.8	4.3	5.6	5.9	10.5	4.2	4.7
1963–64	4.0	6.8	9.8	8.9	9.5	5.2	6.2
1964–65	9.6	3.3	6.3	4.7	9.5	5.0	6.2

¹ Estimates based on gross product at factor cost.
² Included under "Other sectors."
³ Included under "Manufacturing."
Source: UN, *Economic Survey of Latin America, 1965* (New York: 1967).

bia, and Paraguay, but, with the exception of Colombia, the mining sector in these countries is unimportant to the economy as a whole. In Bolivia, where mining accounts for about 13 percent of the GNP, the growth rate decreased from 11 percent in 1964 to 5 percent in 1965. During the same two years in Argentina, Ecuador, Mexico, Peru, and Venezuela production increased 2 to 3 percent. Iron output experienced the most outstanding increase, 25 percent, in 1965.

The manufacturing industry did not influence the relatively high growth rate of Latin America as strongly in 1965 as in 1964. Industrial growth in 1965 was largely supported by Argentina and Brazil, which together account for about 60 percent of Latin America's manufacturing output. The remaining countries experienced a decrease in the growth of manufacturing in 1964, which began to level off after 1965. Part of this decrease has been explained as a result of exhausting the available import-substitution potentials.

The utility sector was the most dynamic component of total gross product, with an average annual growth rate of 10.5 percent in 1960–1965, up from 9.4 percent in 1955–1960. During this period annual growth rates were especially high in Argentina (10 percent) and Venezuela (12 percent). This high growth rate is primarily the result of a larger number of hydroelectric projects under construction, especially in Brazil, Mexico, Chile, Peru, and Venezuela. There has been considerable progress also with respect to the interconnection of electricity networks in the southern regions of South America.

In the transportation sector there has been a movement toward common transportation facilities in air, sea, and land travel throughout the area. This has received substantial support in recent years from several agencies—the International Bank for Reconstruction and Development (IBRD), the Inter-American Development Bank (IDB), and the Agency for International Development (AID). Nevertheless, the cumulative annual growth rate is down from the 1950–1955 high of 5.7 to 4.2 percent for the period 1960–1965.

LAFTA members account for about 90 percent of the gross domestic product of Latin America, and if Venezuela and Bolivia are included the amount increases to 95 percent. In view of the vast difference in gross domestic products (Table 1) and in relation to the increases in intraregional trade, the distribution is not inequitable. Argentina, Brazil, and Mexico account for about 80 percent of the gross domestic product of LAFTA and have experienced 73 percent of the growth in intraregional exports; Ecuador and Paraguay represent 2 percent of the gross domestic product and enjoyed a 4-percent export expansion; and Chile, Colombia, Peru, and Uruguay, with about 20 percent of gross domestic product, have accounted for 22 percent of the intraregional export growth.

FINANCING INTEGRATION

Existing Financial Arrangements

In 1959 the Inter-American Development Bank (IDB) emerged as the "Bank for Integration" and the main multilateral instrument for channeling financial and technical resources to foster the individual and collective growth of Latin America. At its sixth annual meeting in Paraguay, 1965, the Board of Directors of IDB explicitly resolved "to emphasize and provide its broadest possible support for the Bank's effort to expedite and promote the process of Latin American integration."[1] To systematize its actions in the field of integration, two instruments were added to the internal administrative structure of the Bank: (1) the Institute for Latin American Integration (INTAL), 1965, and (2) the Preinvestment Fund for Latin American Integration, 1966.[2]

The functions of INTAL are: (1) to carry out research in various aspects of the integration movement, (2) to train high-level personnel from the private and public sectors engaged in activities actually or potentially related to the integration process, (3) to perform advisory functions with regard to member countries and the Bank itself, and (4) to promote the dissemination of ideas and studies on integration.[3] The Preinvestment Fund, organized to finance preinvestment studies related to multinational and other projects which will contribute to the acceleration of the integration process, concentrates attention on the following areas: (1) multinational infrastructure works, such as high-

---

[1] IDB, *The Inter-American Development Bank and the Economic Integration of Latin America*, p. 15.

[2] Additional steps in the financial sphere, besides the founding of IDB, have been taken in both CACM and LAFTA to establish a payments union and to accept the principle that maintenance of internal policies of stability is a responsibility that should also be regionally approached. In the development financing field, the Central American Bank for Economic Integration (CABEI), created in 1961, has done considerable work, and with the establishment in 1965 of the Central American Fund for Economic Integration under its administration, it is now able to make a further contribution toward building the infrastructure that will accelerate integration.

[3] *Ibid.*, pp. 16–17.

way networks, communications, etc., (2) development of economic regions encompassing more than one country as to energy resources, river navigation, irrigation, etc., (3) development of basic industries on a regional scale, (4) studies related to programs for the joint exploitation of resources, establishment of multinational agencies, etc., and (5) studies related to the institutional and juridical infrastructure of integration.[4]

The Fund operates under the guidance of IDB in consultation with the Secretariat of LAFTA and CACM. Each year programs are reviewed within the framework of the Cómite Interamericano de la Alianza para el Progreso (Inter-American Committee on the Alliance for Progress, CIAP) to assign priorities and provide coordination between planning on the national level and the broad lines of development on the regional level. In general, IDB's activities in the field of integration include such areas as preinvestment and technical assistance, including advisory services to member countries as well as integration agencies, financing of projects, regional development, and planning and training, research, and information.[5]

Table 13 shows, by countries in Latin America, the source of the ordinary capital resources and of the Fund for Special Operations between 1960 and 1965 and the cumulative distributions of loans approved from 1960 to 1964. According to data in this table, LAFTA countries, including Bolivia and Venezuela, account for over 93 percent of the Ordinary Capital Resources funds, and receive about 85 percent of all loans while containing over 90 percent of the population.[6] To some extent, within LAFTA, the collection and distribution of funds has favored the relatively less developed and insufficient-market countries, with about 10 percent of total allocated funds going to the relatively less developed countries (6 percent excluding Bolivia), who contributed less than 4 percent. The countries of insufficient market receive over 33 percent (25 percent excluding Venezuela), while they contributed 30 percent (18 percent excluding Venezuela). The more developed

[4] *Ibid.*, pp. 18–19.

[5] For a complete explanation of these activities see *Ibid.*, pp. 20–26.

[6] The difference between donations and receipts in LAFTA is accounted for by the fact that CACM contains about 6 percent of the population of Latin America but receives over 11 percent of the loans while contributing under 5 percent to the Ordinary Capital Resources Fund.

INTER-AMERICAN DEVELOPMENT BANK—ORDINARY CAPITAL RESOURCES AND FUND FOR SPECIAL OPERATIONS, 1960–1965, AND LOANS APPROVED, CUMULATIVE TO 1964, BY LATIN AMERICAN MEMBERS

Country	Ordinary Capital Resources Fund				Fund for Special Operations		Loans approved					Per capital[1] amount of loans approved
	Paid in	Callable	Total subscribed resources	National percentage of total subscribed resources	Existing quotas	New quotas	Ordinary Capital Resources Fund	Fund for Special Operations	Social Progress Trust Fund	National total of loans approved	National percentage of total loans approved	
	Millions of U.S. dollars				Millions of U.S. dollars		Millions of U.S. dollars					U.S. dollars
LAFTA												
Argentina	51.6	172.9	224.5	22.4	15.5	33.4	91.7	8.6	38.5	138.5	11.9	6.39
Brazil	51.6	172.9	224.5	22.4	15.4	33.4	134.7	31.9	62.0	228.7	19.7	2.99
Mexico	33.2	111.2	144.4	14.4	9.9	21.5	80.5	13.6	30.7	124.8	10.8	3.25
Chile	14.2	47.5	61.7	6.2	4.2	9.2	60.5	8.7	31.9	101.2	8.7	12.34
Colombia	14.2	47.4	61.6	6.2	4.2	9.2	51.2	3.2	49.4	103.8	8.9	6.87
Peru	6.9	23.2	30.1	3.0	2.1	4.5	16.8	.4	36.0	53.2	4.6	4.84
Uruguay	5.5	18.5	23.0	2.6	1.1	3.6	19.4	4.2	10.5	34.2	2.9	13.15
Venezuela	27.6	92.6	120.2	12.0	8.3	17.9	30.7	2.7	63.0	96.4	8.2	11.90
Bolivia	4.1	13.9	18.0	1.8	1.2	2.7		26.6	11.3	37.9	3.2	10.53
Ecuador	2.8	9.3	12.1	1.2	.8	1.8	8.3	8.5	24.8	41.6	3.6	8.85
Paraguay	2.1	6.9	9.0	.9	.6	1.3	2.8	22.6	6.3	31.7	2.7	16.68
CACM												
Costa Rica	2.1	6.9	9.0	.9	.6	1.3	11.5	1.0	12.6	25.1	2.1	19.31
El Salvador	2.1	6.9	9.0	.9	.6	1.3	4.0	.1	16.0	20.2	1.7	7.48
Guatemala	2.8	9.3	12.1	1.2	.8	1.8	8.4	.5	14.3	23.3	2.1	5.68
Honduras	2.1	6.9	9.0	.9	.6	1.3	.5	9.4	7.6	17.6	1.5	8.80
Nicaragua	2.1	6.9	9.0	.9	.6	1.3	8.9	4.5	13.1	26.6	2.3	17.73
Central America								14.2	2.9	17.1	1.4	....
OTHER												
Panama	2.1	6.9	9.0	.9	.6	1.3	8.5	4.2	10.4	23.1	2.0	19.25
Dominican Republic	2.8	9.3	12.1	1.2	.8	1.8	6.0	...	8.6	14.6	1.2	4.42
Total	229.9	769.4	999.3	100.0	67.9	147.6	544.4	164.9	449.9	1159.9	100.0	5.53

[1] Computed on the basis of 1963 population statistics.

Source: Developed from U.S. Bureau of the Census, *Statistical Abstract of the U.S., 1965* (Washington, D.C.: 1965), p. 946.

countries—Argentina, Brazil, and Mexico—contributed 59 percent of the total Latin American contribution but received only 42 percent.[7] A similar situation is found when the distribution is looked at in terms of the amount allocated per person. For example, the average amount allocated per capita between 1950 and 1964 was 4.20 dollars for the more developed countries, 9.80 dollars for the insufficient-market countries, and 12.00 dollars for the relatively less developed countries.

More recent developments in the financing of integration occurred with the Declaration of the Presidents of America and the Action Plan of Viña del Mar. Here it was stated that the process of Latin American economic integration, in progressing toward the Common Market, will need funds in addition to those now made available to the countries for supporting economic development. In accordance with these decisions, proposals on the financing of integration are to be submitted to the next Inter-American Economic and Social Council (IA-ECOSOC) meeting sometime in mid-1968. It is also recommended that CIAP coordinate and promote the necessary work to present the studies and proposals to the Second Meeting of Government Representatives on the Financing of Latin American Economic Integration in May 1968.

The guidelines for orienting the work of these experts are as follows: (1) financing of the balance of payments and the expansion of trade (which includes a system of compensating reciprocal balance and credits and financing of transitory imbalances and possible use of a common fund); (2) financing to offset a transitory drop in overall fiscal revenues as a result of the integration process; (3) financing of the reconversion of industry and orientation of manpower; and (4) financing of studies, projects, and programs related to integration (which includes financing the preparation as well as multinational projects related to infrastructure, sectoral, or complementation agreements, integrated regional development programs, etc., and the financ-

[7] The trend is slowly moving more in favor of the relatively less developed and insufficient-market countries. According to data on Social Progress Fund loans, between 1961 and 1966, about 10 percent of the total funds went to the relatively less developed countries (7 percent excluding Bolivia), 44 percent of the total went to the countries of insufficient market (29 percent excluding Venezuela), and about 28 percent of all funds were allocated to the more developed group—Argentina, Brazil, and Mexico.

ing of studies related to transforming the present organization of LAFTA and CACM into one common market).[8]

Intraregional Financing

Many associate heavy financial outlay with a program on integration: not only are projects costly in the aggregate, but the seriousness of effort itself depends on the adequacy of backing. Others in fundamental agreement as to probable costliness contend, however, that financing poses no immediate constraint; sufficient financing to service current activity is available, they suggest, or can be made available, through existing arrangements—through, say, the IDB or like institutions.

Yet, even if financing seems adequate in some overall sense, can it be regarded as adequate also in terms of the needs of the relatively less developed countries? It is possible that available financing will, in the absence of special arrangements to the contrary, simply come to be applied very largely in the countries already more developed. If such is a strong likelihood there is then a case for evolving supplementary procedures that can give the less developed countries a better prospect for new production facilities. Needless to say, not only is there reason to believe that something further along these lines is needed to place the less developed countries more nearly on a par with more developed countries, but a body of thought already exists as to the form this support might take.

One approach, perhaps thought of only in terms of initial application solely within the LAFTA area, is to establish a special "integration fund" on behalf of development in the less developed countries. Contributions would come from all members—computed, say, as a small percentage of current GNP. Eligibility for financing, on a loan basis, would extend to projects in less developed countries, and to those multinational projects involving directly one or more of the less de-

[8] For a more detailed explanation of these guidelines see Pan American Union (IA-ECOSOC), *Meeting of Government Representatives on the Financial Implications of Latin American Integration,* and Pan American Union (IA-ECOSOC), *Final Report of the Meeting of Working Group II of Governmental Experts for Study of the Financial Implications of Latin American Integration.*

veloped countries. Administration could be by the IDB, already widely referred to as the "Bank of Integration."

Ostensibly two main advantages could derive from such an arrangement. First, less developed countries could reasonably envisage enhanced developmental potential for themselves, and, hence, would feel greater enthusiasm in their overall participation. Second, all countries would stand to be drawn together more closely, thereby strengthening the basic integration spirit.

EVALUATION AND CONJECTURE

LAFTA has encountered problems far more formidable than has CACM, not so much because of any difference in diligence of effort, but more directly because of a difference in environment. The contrast in the two experiences has provided the lesson that diversity invites disunity and that this situation, unless countered, impairs the very basis for successful integration.

The success of LAFTA to date makes feasible the 1985 target date set by the Declaration of the Presidents of America for the establishment of a common market for all Latin America. As seen in Part I of this report, a number of formidable problems stood in the path of economic integration. A strong rationale, however, a desire for economic development, and an innovative spirit, as seen in Part II, resulted in LAFTA's bypassing many of these roadblocks. The past achievements and success of economic integration are truly praiseworthy; continued success and eventual establishment of a LACM, however, depend on how quickly several issues are resolved.

Foreign Influence

It is now the common belief among many Latin Americans and other development economists that the economic integration of Latin America and the formation of a LACM is the best means to promote economic development. The emphasis once placed on foreign aid is fading as the developing countries find that developed countries are less willing to make additional commitments because of domestic problems, and as their burden of debt servicing continues to rise.

Figure 14, showing the evolution of foreign aid, trade, and investment in Latin America, contains some important implications for future policy. As total foreign aid from the United States (the major source of aid) to the world began to decrease in 1951[1] foreign trade of

---

[1] Between 1955 and 1961 the distribution of U.S. foreign aid moved in favor of Latin America at the expense of Europe and the Far East, but thereafter it leveled off, falling victim to the generally decreasing trend in U.S. foreign assistance.

Figure 14

LATIN AMERICA: EVOLUTION OF FOREIGN AID, TRADE AND INVESTMENT, 1948-1966

Millions of U.S. dollars   Millions of U.S. dollars

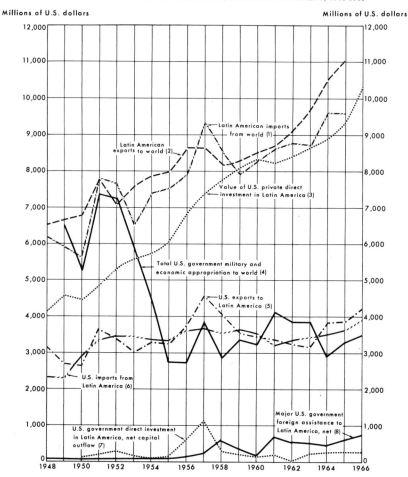

Source: (1) and (2) UN, *Statistical Yearbook* (New York, 1959-1965—various issues); (3) U.S. Department
of Commerce, *Balance of Payments, Statistical Supplement* (Washington: 1963), pp. 208-209, and U.S.
Bureau of the Census, *Statistical Abstract of the U.S., 1966* (Washington: 1966) p. 858; (4) Agency
for International Development, *Proposed Mutual Defense and Development Programs FY 1966*
(Washington: 1965), p. 1; (5) and (6) U.S. Department of Commerce, *Business Statistics* (Washington:
1967), pp. 111 and 116; (7) U.S. Department of Commerce, *Balance of Payments, Statistical Supplement*
(Washington: 1963), p. 176, and U.S. Department of Commerce, *Survey of Current Business* (Washington:
September 1967), p. 45; (8) U.S. Bureau of the Census, *Statistical Abstract of the U.S., 1966*
(Washington: 1966), p. 865, and U.S. Department of Commerce, *Foreign Aid by the U.S. Government,
1940-1951* (Washington: 1952), p. 36.

Latin America with the United States and the world continued to increase rapidly until 1957. Between 1957 and 1960 Latin American trade with the United States and the world decreased until 1961, when this trend changed as trade with the world expanded rapidly. Outstanding is the persistent upward trend of U.S. private direct investment in Latin America, especially since 1957.

As foreign aid continues to fall it is being replaced with expanding foreign trade. Maintaining their traditional exports of raw material, the developing countries of Latin America are diversifying their production and exporting more new products in constantly increasing amounts. Along with this expansion of extraregional trade has come an expansion of intraregional trade. Efforts to continue to stimulate foreign trade are being made to force a change in the existing rules of trade—a breaking down of the philosophy of GATT— in favor of new rules of trade being considered at the United Nations Conference on Trade and Development (UNCTAD) meetings.[2] At the same time it is realized that the dependence on foreign trade will and should be removed if the developing countries of Latin America are to industrialize and develop. In this respect efforts have progressed well to industrialize the domestic economy by setting up different types of infant industries—both import-substitution and export-creation industries.

The establishment of a common external tariff will make it profitable for foreign firms to invest within the region rather than attempt to compete—via trade from outside the region—with sheltered domestic industries located within the region. Therefore, pursuit of the establishment of a common market will raise fears and actual barriers against foreign goods competing with domestic production and thus compel foreign investment to flow into the region stimulating economic activity. The next element in our policy triad then is the important displacement of foreign trade by foreign investment.

---

[2] At the first United Nations Conference on Trade and Development (UNCTAD) meeting, in 1964, the developing countries presented a united front and, after attacking the old order, called for a restructuring of existing trade and for production in favor of the developing countries or a retransfer of income back to developing countries. The second UNCTAD meeting, in 1968 in New Delhi, attempted to formalize the restructuring of tariffs in developed countries to favor manufactured products exported from developing countries. The meeting, however, failed to accomplish its objectives.

For U.S. business the implications of the establishment of a single common market in Latin America are changing trade patterns which would provide new competition at home and abroad and would alter investment flows because of the need for U.S. business to invest inside the common market. Although the attitude of the United States toward Latin America is changing, as witnessed at the Meeting of Presidents in 1967, additional changes are required if the United States is to meet the challenge of LACM.

The United States attitude before the meeting of the Presidents in April was one of involvement and encouragement for CACM—financially and otherwise. However, it was not until President Johnson signed the Declaration of Punta del Este, in April 1967, that the United States showed any signs of encouragement to LAFTA and a LACM—which several years earlier it had been opposed to. The general feeling at LAFTA since the meeting of the Presidents is that there has been a significant change in U.S. foreign policy toward Latin America as evidenced by President Johnson's statement that the United States would give monetary and moral support to the development of a LACM. Nevertheless, our foreign-aid program has not yet been modified to encourage multinational projects or regional development. Foreign aid, rather, is still distributed and managed on a bilateral basis.[3]

Another important possible development in U.S. policy is indicated by former Undersecretary of State George Ball's statement that the United States may have to make trade preferences for Latin America similar to those made by EEC for African countries.[4] The United States has recently increased its contributions by $150 million to the IDB in line with the President's statements at the Punta del Este meeting. In an adverse mood, the preliminary vote by the Senate's Foreign Relations Committee was to cut U.S. aid to Latin America from $643 million to $578 million for 1968. This cut was criticized by Dr. Carlos Sanz de Santamaría, chairman of the Inter-American Committee on

[3] The United States has no official representation in LAFTA, naturally, but it does have an unofficial representative in Montevideo, W. V. Turnage, who reports to Washington.

[4] A similar statement was made by Canada's Prime Minister Lester Pearson, who called for new tariff negotiations to make it easier for developing countries to sell their products to the richer countries.

the Alliance for Progress, who said that this action would endanger the time table for creating a Latin American Common Market.

Other recent occurrences are that the United States requested permission to sit in as an observer on the Council of Ministers meeting in August 1967. When this matter was brought before the representatives of the LAFTA countries permission was denied. This attitude seemed to strengthen LAFTA's desire to go it alone without U.S. interference. A change of mind, however, if not a softening of policy, was revealed after the Council of Ministers meeting in the form of an agreement passed to create a committee to work out mutual problems and perhaps act as spokesman for LAFTA in the United States and Europe.[5]

Current Status and Future Prospects

The problems of LAFTA within a nine-country context are a matter of record. For the future it seems only reasonable to expect somewhat similar problems on a greater scale as the movement to a full LACM proceeds. The major problems, rooted in diversity, do not, of course, rest fundamentally with the more advanced countries; these countries are moving ahead, and stand to move ahead even faster as the benefits of integration accrue. The existent problem is rather with the less developed countries, and, while there can be no true regional integration without them, cooperation on their part presumes "adequate" benefits for them as well as for the more advanced countries.

During the recent Council of Ministers meeting of LAFTA it became increasingly evident that the primary bottleneck currently impeding the establishment of LACM is the status of the less developed countries. Indecision by the Council of Ministers reflected less than all-out support for economic integration by the LAFTA members. Involved were conflicts of interest between the less developed and the relatively more developed countries over (1) the pace of the integration process, (2) the extent of integration, and (3) the distribution of the benefits of integration. The first two points are obviously related directly to the third point involving the general aim of balanced development or reciprocity.[6]

[5] See *New York Times*, September 1, 1967, p. 23.

[6] Reciprocity is defined as the sanctioning of greater benefits for the less developed countries by the more developed countries than the benefits expected by the more developed countries for themselves.

The primary problem is defining balanced development—or reciprocity—within the present framework of integration, and its meaning in relation to a future LACM. There are essentially two approaches to benefit distribution among countries: an equal distribution of benefits, or a granting of a greater than proportional amount of benefits for the less developed countries. Overlapping both approaches is the question of what index should be used to measure benefits: per capita income, GNP, intrazonal trade, degree of industrialization, etc.—one or all of them?

In the case of CACM, resolutions stress an equal distribution of benefits, whereas emphasis by the Central American Bank for Economic Integration is on the granting of greater benefits to the less developed countries. Because of the high degree of similarity among the Central American countries, in contrast to the diversity among the LAFTA members, the difference between the two approaches is negligible for CACM. In the case of LAFTA, documentation of views of the Conference and of the Council of Ministers shows, contradictorily, that both desire, in some degree, an equal distribution of benefits and in other cases greater than proportional benefits for the less developed countries.

This problem of balanced development is an issue because of the diverse economies of members of LAFTA. The relatively less developed and insufficient-market countries expect from the more developed countries special concessions that will guarantee them a share of the gains of industrialization. They expect this as a condition of participation in the integration process and the opening of their markets to intrazonal trade and competition. Conversely, Argentina, Brazil, and Mexico face the problem of comparing the cost of integration (the amount of new industrialization that must be given to the less developed countries) with the benefits accruing to them (expanded markets through free intrazonal trade).

Within this framework the less developed countries stand to gain, merely by being members of the Common Market, in the following ways:

(1) Imports already arising within the region will be acquired more cheaply—as duties are lowered and as greater efficiency is fostered throughout the region (probably yielding lower prices than otherwise to be expected). The end consumer stands to benefit, as do those produc-

ers dependent upon imports from within the region for some facet of production carried on by them.

(2) Those forms of economic activity in which the countries have a comparative advantage within the region can be expected to be aided as eased access to a regional market is obtained. The impact upon these forms of economic activity is likely to prove conducive to the generation of higher income and employment.

(3) Increased mobility of the factors of production within the region can be expected to "draw off" some "surplus" labor from countries of lesser development to countries of greater development, and is likely also to ease access to the more abundant capital supplies of countries of greater development. In short, distinctive pressure toward income equalization (rather than a relative widening in differentials) can be expected. In a sense the major countries within the region will set the pace of regional economic activity while the smaller countries (of less development) will be "carried along" by the overall regional influence.

(4) All the while, the countries of lesser development, primarily raw-materials producers (and generally specialized raw-materials producers of one or few main products) will be unaffected, for all practical purposes, in their capacities to enter markets outside the Common Market area.

However, the several drawbacks for the countries of lesser development include the following:

(1) Government revenues can be expected to experience at least a momentary hardship as duties on intraregional trade are foregone. Although the same can be said for countries of greater development, a consideration is at issue which merits attention.

(2) The countries will undoubtedly need to forego the "ideal" of diversified natural development, since they would be committing themselves to a course in which economic improvement is sought via integration within an economic framework in reference to which other member countries presumably carry more economic weight. A case can be made, of course, that—in terms of overall economic efficiency and general economic well-being—this is as it ought to be. The same statement also can be made of the more developed members of the Common Market area, but for these other countries the reorientation in emphasis is virtually certain to prove less drastic in impact.

The implication invited by these facts is that the less developed countries within the region will tend to remain in that relative status (relative to the more developed countries within the region)—at least insofar as regional integration may hope to affect the situation. The less developed countries, however, will tend to gain from regional integration (that is, will tend to be better off economically than if their economic destinies were planned solely in unilateral terms.) This is at least the minimum that can be expected from integration by the less developed countries.[7]

The prescription here is that the leaders of integration, as they push to hasten the transformation to a LACM, should be presently concerned with the status of the less developed countries. In this connection, and in order to add to and improve upon the minimum referred to above, five areas of potential activity seem to merit special attention: (1) the exercise of leadership (apropos the role of the Council of Ministers of LAFTA), (2) subregional (that is, CACM, the Andean Group, and the River Plata Agreement) and sector integration (complementation agreements), (3) intraregional trade and the automatic tariff-reduction system, (4) the common external tariff, and (5) intraregional financing. Although the importance of each of these has been extensively discussed in Part II, the need here is to emphasize that the developments in these areas will determine the future of the less developed countries and hence the success of a Latin American Common Market.

---

[7] For an earlier appraisal along these lines, see Walter Krause, *The Impact of the Latin American Common Market on the Economies of Member States of the Organization of American States*. Further analysis of the situation of the relatively less developed countries in a LACM is given in Walter Krause and F. John Mathis, *The Latin American Common Market: Economic Disparity and Benefit Diffusion*.

BIBLIOGRAPHY

Agency for International Development. *Proposed Mutual Defense and Development Programs FY 1966.* Washington: 1965.

Balassa, Bela. *The Theory of Economic Integration.* Homewood, Illinois: Richard D. Irwin, 1961.

Blough, Roy, Jack N. Behrman, and Romulo A. Ferrero. *Regional Integration and the Trade of Latin America.* New York: Committee for Economic Development, 1968.

Buenos Aires Herald, August 10, 1967.

Business International. LAFTA: *Key to Latin America's 200 Million Consumers.* New York: June 1966.

———. "Building a Common Outer Tariff Raises Complex Issues for LAFTA Study Group," *Business Latin America.* New York: June 1, 1967.

———. *Business Latin America.* New York: July 6, 1967.

———. *Business Latin America.* New York: July 13, 1967.

———. "Laftagram," *Business Latin America.* New York: July 20, 1967.

Dell, Sidney. *A Latin American Common Market?* London: Oxford University Press, 1966.

Frei, Eduardo. "Integración de America Latina," *Progreso 66/67.* New York: Vision, 1967.

Inter-American Development Bank. *The Inter-American Development Bank and the Economic Integration of Latin America.* Washington: 1966.

Johnson, Harry G. *The World Economy at the Crossroads.* London: Oxford University Press, 1965.

Krause, Walter. *The Impact of Latin American Common Markets on the Economies of Member States of the Organization of American States.* Washington: Pan American Union, 1959. Staff paper.

Krause, Walter, and F. John Mathis. *The Latin American Common Market: Economic Disparity and Benefit Diffusion.* Atlanta: Bureau of Business and Economic Research, Georgia State College, June 1968.

Latin American Free Trade Association. *Sintesis Mensual.* Montevideo: October 1965.

———. *Sintesis Mensual.* Montevideo: December 1965.

———. *Sintesis Mensual.* Montevideo: January 1967.

———. *Sintesis Mensual.* Montevideo: July 1967.

———. *Sintesis Mensual.* Montevideo: October 1967.

———. *Sintesis Mensual.* Montevideo: December 1967.

——— (Comisión Asesara de Desarrollo Industrial). *Informe de la Secretaría sobre las Resultados del Grupo de Estudio de la Industria Siderurgica,* ALALC/CADI/III/dt. 4. Montevideo: September 2, 1966.

———. (Comisión Asesara de Desarrollo Industrial). *Informe de la Secretaría sobre las Resultados del Grupo de Estudio sobre las Industrias Quimicas Derivadas del Petroleo,* ALALC/CADI/III/dt. 6. Montevideo: October 7, 1966.

———. (Comisión Asesora de Desarrollo Industrial). *Informe Final de la Tercera Reunión de la Comisión Asesora de Desarrollo Industrial,* ALALC/CADI/III/Informe. Montevideo: June 30, 1967.

———. (Comisión Asesora de Asuntos Monetarios). *Financiamiento del Balance de Pagos y la Ampliación del Credito Comercial,* ALALC/CAM/ V/di 2/Rev. 1. Montevideo: December 12, 1967.

———. (Cómite Ejecutivo Permanente). *Resoluciones.* Montevideo: 1966.

———. (Cómite Ejecutivo Permanente). *Resolución 104.* Montevideo: October 20, 1966.

———. (Cómite Ejecutivo Permanente). *Acta de la Reunión de la Comisión Ad-Hoc de la Asociación Latinoamericana de Libre Comercio y los Organos Ejecutivos del Mercado Común Centroamericano,* CEP/Repartido 871. Montevideo: 1967.

———. (Cómite Ejecutivo Permanente). ALALC *Comercio Intrazonal Primer Quinquento del Tratado de Montevideo, 1962–1966,* CEP/Repartido 787. Montevideo: March 14, 1967.

———. (Cómite Ejecutivo Permanente). *Restricciones Aplicables a la Importación de Mercaderías Vigentes en los Paises de la* ALALC, CEP/ Repartido 820/Rev. 1. Montevideo: June 13, 1967.

———. (Cómite Ejecutivo Permanente). *Derechos Aduaneros y Gravamenes de Efectos Equivalentes Aplicables a la Importación de Mercaderías, Vigentes en los Paises de la* ALALC, CEP/Repartido 819/Rev. 1. Montevideo: June 14, 1967.

———. (Cómite Ejecutivo Permanente). *Comercio Intrazonal por Paises de Destino o Procedencia,* CEP/Repartido 876/Add. 1. Montevideo: August 14, 1967.

———. (Conferencia). *Resoluciones.* Montevideo: 1966.

———. (Council of Ministers). *Resolución 170* (CM-I/II-E). Montevideo: December 10, 1966.

———. Working Paper, CEP/GE. AEC/I/1. Montevideo: May 3, 1967.

Machinery and Allied Products Institute. *The Latin American Free Trade Association: Progress and Prospects.* Washington: May 11, 1967.

The New York Times, September 1, 1967.

————, September 5, 1967.

Pan American Union. *Latin America's Foreign Trade.* Washington: 1966.

————. (IA-ECOSOC). *Meeting of Government Representatives on the Financial Implications of Latin American Integration.* Washington: October 3, 1967.

————. (IA-ECOSOC). *Final Report of the Meeting of Working Group II of Governmental Experts for Study of the Financial Implications of Latin American Integration.* Washington: March 6, 1968.

Time, September 15, 1967.

Turnage, W. V. LAFTA *1966 in Review.* Montevideo: 1967. Mimeographed report.

————. LAFTA *Notes.* Montevideo: 1967. Mimeographed report.

————. LAFTA *Tariff Concessions and Zonal Trade.* Montevideo: 1967. Mimeographed report.

————. "Unstable Currencies Hamper LAFTA Trade Growth, Cloud Picture for U.S. Traders and Investors," *International Commerce.* Washington: September 25, 1967.

————. LAFTA *Developments (1967).* Montevideo: 1968. Mimeographed report.

————. *Seventh* LAFTA *Conference (1967).* Montevideo: 1968. Mimeographed report.

United Nations. *Monthly Bulletin of Statistics.* New York (various issues).

————. *Yearbook of International Trade Statistics.* New York (various issues).

————. *The Economic Development of Latin America and Its Principal Problems.* New York: 1950.

————. *Study of Inter-Latin American Trade.* New York: 1957.

————. *Economic Survey of Latin America, 1965.* New York: 1967.

————. *Statistical Yearbook, 1966.* New York: 1967.

United States Bureau of the Census. *Statistical Abstract of the U.S., 1965.* Washington: 1965.

————. *Statistical Abstract of the U.S., 1966.* Washington: 1966.

United States Department of Commerce. *Foreign Aid by the U.S. Government.* Washington: 1952.

111

———. *Balance of Payments, Statistical Supplement.* Washington: 1963.
———. *Business Statistics.* Washington: 1966.
———. *Survey of Current Business.* Washington: September 1967.
U.S. Department of State Bulletin. Washington: May 8, 1967.
University of California at Los Angeles (Latin American Center). *Statistical Abstract of Latin America, 1965.* Los Angeles: 1966.
Viner, Jacob. *The Customs Union Issue.* New York: Carnegie Endowment for International Peace, 1950.
Wionczek, Miguel S. (ed.). *Latin American Economic Integration.* New York: Frederick A. Praeger, 1966.

DATE DUE

MAY 17 1972		
MAY 1 0 1975 DEC 1 8 1984		
MAY 20 1991		
GAYLORD		PRINTED IN U.S.A.